#1 Book to Learn Microsoft Copilot

The Ultimate Beginner's Guide to Mastering AI

By: Heather Matalski

Written in Edmonton, Alberta, Canada.
For more information, contact: Matalski.heather@outlook.com

Book design by Heather Matalski
Cover design by Heather Matalski

ISBN# 9798316500765
Second Edition: April 2025

Dedication

To my 4 wonderful children, who inspire and
encourage me everyday

Table of Contents

Introduction

Hello, and welcome to my newest book, "The Best Way to Learn Microsoft Copilot'. I'm so glad you've joined me today to discover what Copilot is and what it can do for you!

This book will introduce you to a whole new way to get things done! Microsoft's AI-powered chat feature, called Copilot, is not just a fancy new chatbot; it is a revolutionary new tool that will transform the way you do, well, almost everything. You might be thinking that it's just a search engine or browser, but it's more than that. This Copilot feature is like having an AI for a best friend who helps you find answers to anything; it generates original content just for you and unlocks your creativity in its simple chat interface.

Copilot uses its AI power to deliver better chat experiences. It gives you better results, more complete answers, and personalized suggestions. You can ask short or long, specific or vague questions, and it will reply to you in a very natural conversational way. It can follow up on what you previously chatted about and keep the conversation going.

Besides being your new best friend — yes, that is a real thing, Copilot can be used as a creative assistant to help you create amazing original content. With just a few words, it can produce an original poem, short story, or even code for you programmers out there. You want to create a meme, make a collage, or design a logo? All you must do is ask. It can even improve your written content by summarizing, editing, or completely rewriting it.

Another cool thing about Copilot is that there are also ways to make money with it. By this, I mean that whatever answer, image, or idea, for example, it gives you, you can use for products or services you want to sell. For example, you can use Copilot to write code for you that you can turn around and use in web or mobile application development that you can sell to clients or customers. You can also make digital or physical products and sell them using images, jokes, and so much more that Copilot generates.

Microsoft has spent years on AI research and innovation to produce one of the best AI technologies out there. It was developed using the latest version of OpenAI 'LLM technology' and was created by Microsoft to support users in various other Microsoft 365 applications, like Excel, Teams, and Outlook, for example. For those with technical knowledge, Copilot uses advanced natural language processing, computer vision, deep learning, and generative models to understand your needs and produce high-quality content.

In other words, Copilot uses computer skills, like understanding how words work, seeing things like images, and learning from lots of examples, so it can create top-notch content just for you. It also follows the principles of responsible AI to ensure your data is secure, private, and compliant with your preferences.

Copilot is available now as a built-in feature in the Microsoft Edge browser and at www.copilot/Microsoft.com. Just so you know, it used to be called Bing Copilot or Bing Enterprise recently, but it goes by Microsoft Copilot or just Copilot now. The basic version of Copilot is free, but Copilot 365 charges you a subscription fee. This version offers more advanced features and security for work-related tasks.

So, as you can see, Copilot is a game changer in the way we search the web and create content. It opens new possibilities for productivity, learning, entertainment, and self-expression while making the web more easily accessible, engaging, and fun for everyone.

This book is your comprehensive beginners guide to the free version of Copilot, and it's written in an easy-to-understand language. It will teach you the basics of Copilot and how to use it effectively and productively. It will show you how to customize some of Copilot's features and settings to your own needs.

This book is full of tips, tricks, and other useful information to make the most of Copilot. So don't worry; I've got you covered. By the time you reach the end of this book, you'll have a thorough understanding of how to use Copilot to enhance both your personal and professional life. Along the way, I promise you'll experience plenty of fun and creative moments. I sincerely hope you enjoy reading this book as much as I enjoyed writing it.

Now, let's dive in!

CHAPTER 1

Getting Started with Copilot

Welcome to the world of Copilot! In this chapter, we will be covering the basics. Knowing how to access Copilot is the first step. There are a few ways to do this, which I'll show you. Then I'll Walk you through the different prompts (questions or queries) you can input into Copilot to interact with it. We will also be going over some basic features and settings to give you a clear understanding of the options available to you and how to use them.

By the end of this chapter, you will have a solid grasp of how to access Copilot, prompt it for your desired responses, explore its features, and use it effectively with confidence.
Accessing Copilot is an easy, straightforward process. To begin using Copilot's limitless features, it can be accessed through a web browser, the Bing mobile app, or the Microsoft Edge browser.

You will need to have a Microsoft account and be signed in to use Copilot. In the Microsoft Edge browser, click on the Copilot icon in the top right corner. This will open Copilot in a docked side window, and it's ready to use. Or you can go to www.copilot/microsoft.com, where it will ask you to sign into your Microsoft account to get started. Other ways to access Copilot are:

Using a Web Browser

-   Open your preferred web browser (Chrome, Firefox, Safari, etc.)

-   In the search bar, type "Bing Co-pilot" or navigate directly to the Bing website.

-   Look for the co-pilot feature; typically, it may be accessible through a dedicated section, an icon, or a chat-like interface.

-   Click on the co-pilot icon or chat window to initiate the interaction. Some versions might require signing in to your Microsoft or Bing account for full access.

Copilot's Mobile App

-   Download and install the Copilot app from the respective app store (Google Play Store for Android or Apple App Store for iOS).

-   Open the app on your mobile device.

-   Look for the co-pilot feature within the app interface.

- Tap on the co-pilot icon or chat window to start using the feature. Ensure you are logged into your Microsoft or Bing account for seamless access.

Note: Accessing Copilot may vary slightly based on updates, device configuration, or regional availability. Copilot isn't available in China (excluding Hong Kong SAR and Taiwan) or Russia, but both the simplified Chinese and Russian languages are supported.

Now that you know Copilot is just a few clicks away, it's time to open it up and explore some of its options. Now, as I previously mentioned, Copilot may vary depending on the way it's been accessed. For example, there are small differences between the Copilot you open in a docked window on the side and the actual full-page Copilot website. The options are minor, but they are there.

- Clicking on the Copilot icon in the top right corner opens a docked side window pane where you will see these options and icons that I've explained in more detail below. At the top of the pane, there are three icons: Chat, Compose, and Insights tab:

- Chat: This is the default mode in Copilot where you can have natural conversations, ask questions, and request tasks.

- Compose: This mode lets you use Copilot as a writing assistant. Type in a topic, genre, prompt, or partial text, and it will generate more on the subject, continue, or complete the text for you. You can edit the generated text and request more suggestions.

- Insights: This mode allows you to get feedback or insights from Copilot or your chat history. You can see how your messages were rated, what emotions they detected, and what topics they identified. You can also get Copilot to summarize or analyze your chat history.

To the right of these three icons, you will see:

- Open the link in the new page: This opens Copilot on a new full page, which looks a little different than the side window pane. For example, it does not have the Summarize webpage option because it is a full page. Only the smaller side window pane has this option. This is because it summarizes the webpage you are viewing.

- Refresh button: Gives you a new, fresh chat

- Three little dots: Has additional options for you to customize your Copilot experience.

- Exit icon: Closes the side Copilot window.

The next three options you will see, located in the middle of the Copilot docked side window pane, are three modes for you to choose from. These modes are balanced, creative, and precise. You can switch between these modes anytime you like by clicking on them. Each mode has a different style and tone of communication, as well as its own separate features and capabilities.

Balanced Mode: This is the default mode of Copilot. It's designed to provide helpful, informative, and engaging responses that are neither too formal nor too casual. Balanced mode can perform a variety of tasks, such as summarizing web pages, generating images, comparing products, answering questions, and more.

Creative Mode: This is the mode that unleashes the full potential of Copilot's imagination and innovation. It can create original and entertaining content such as poems, stories, code, songs, essays, rewritten content, or improve or optimize your own written works.

Precise Mode: This is the mode that focuses on accuracy and clarity. It provides factual, concise, and objective responses that are based on reliable sources and data. This mode can also help you with complex queries, such as mathematical calculations, scientific explanations, historical facts, and more.

When Copilot is open in the docked side window, you will see under the Balanced, Creative, and Precise options a button that says, 'Generate page summary". This button will give you a brief overview of any page you have opened in the Microsoft Edge Browser, it helps save you time and helps you understand the main points of a page without reading the whole thing. You can just click on this button or type into the chat box 'What is this page about?' and you will receive a summary with references to the source. You can further ask for more details or refine the summary by providing more context.

Engaging with Copilot

Once Copilot is open, interacting with it is simple and straightforward; just type in your query into the chat box for a response or guidance. You can also use your voice by clicking on the microphone icon in the chat box interface.

To ask a question, simply type or speak your question into the chat box. You can use natural language and ask your question in a conversational way. For example, you can ask, "What's the weather like today?" or "How do you say I'm hungry in French?". You can also use keywords and phrases to narrow down your query. For example, you can ask "Weather in New York" or "Translate 'How are you' to Spanish".

Once you ask it a question, it will process your query and search for the best answer from various sources. It will answer your question in the chat interface. Depending on the type and complex nature of your question, the answer may vary in format and length. For example, if you ask a simple factual question, such as "Who is the president of the United States?" you will get a short and direct answer.

If you ask a more complex or open-ended question, such as "What are the benefits of meditation?" Copilot will give you a longer and more detailed answer, such as "Meditation can help you reduce stress, improve focus, enhance mood, and more.

There is also the option to 'Speak' your request by clicking on the 'use microphone' button or upload an image request by clicking the 'add image' icon, both of which are located in the chat box. Exploring your copilot's settings also offers customization options for personal preferences and language settings to make it a more personalized interaction.

It's important to understand that while Copilot strives to provide helpful information, it's crucial to cross-verify critical or sensitive information to ensure it's from a reliable and credible source for added safety and accuracy.

The Different Types of Prompts

Now that you have Copilot open, let's look at some examples of different prompts you can input into the chat interface to get various answers.

Text Input

How to: Type a question directly into the chat interface.
Result: Copilot provides relevant information or guidance based on the question entered.

Voice Input

How to: Use voice commands or the microphone icon (if available) to speak your question aloud.
Result: The co-pilot converts your speech to text and generates responses or answers based on the spoken question.

Image Upload

How to: Look for an image upload icon within the chat box and click to upload an image.

Result: Co-pilot utilizes image recognition technology to analyze the uploaded image and provide information or related content based on the image content.

Link Sharing

How to: Paste a URL or share a link within the chat box.
Result: The co-pilot may provide relevant information,
summaries, or previews related to the shared link's content.

Emojis or symbols

How to: Use emojis or special symbols within the chat box.
Result: The co-pilot may interpret and respond to certain
emojis or symbols based on their meanings or context.

Location-based queries

How to: Provide location-based questions, such as asking for
nearby restaurants, attractions, or weather.

Result: The co-pilot offers information relevant to the specified
location, such as restaurant recommendations, local
attractions, or current weather conditions.

Date and time queries

How to: Input your question related to dates or times, such as
asking for upcoming events, historical dates, or time zone
information.

Result: The co-pilot provides responses based on the date or
time- related question, offering event details, historical
information, or time zone conversions.

Mathematical and Conversion Questions

How to: Enter mathematical equations or conversion questions
(e.g., currency conversions, unit conversions).

Result: The co-pilot calculates mathematical equations or converts units or currencies, displaying the results.

Personalized Question

How to: Include personal details or preferences in your question, such as asking for tailored recommendations based on interests or past interactions.

Result: The co-pilot uses the provided personal information to offer customized suggestions, recommendations, or advice.

Follow-up Questions

How to: Ask follow-up questions or continue a conversation based on previous interactions with the co-pilot.

Result: The co-pilot maintains context from previous conversations and provides continuity in responses or additional information related to the ongoing discussion. Each of the methods above for entering prompts caters to different forms of communication you can have with Copilot.

The preferences you set and the questions you ask allow you to have a personalized interaction with Copilot. The results will vary, and they also depend on the input method used, with Copilot striving to provide helpful and relevant information every time.

CHAPTER 2

Entering Specific Commands

Another great feature of Copilot is that you do not need to type in a complete question each time you are looking for answers. You can also input 'One word' commands into the chat interface, which allows you to execute specific tasks, get information, or perform calculations.

These specific commands, which we go into more detail about, are recognized by Copilot for particular functions. Copilot executes the requested function or provides relevant information to the command used. Here are some examples of what I mean.

"Translate [word or phrase] to [language]": This command translates a specified word or phrase to the desired language.
- Example: "Translate hello to French."

"Define [word]": This command provides the definition of the specified word.
- Example: "Define ubiquitous."

"Weather in [location]": Retrieves the current weather conditions for the specified location.
- Example: "Weather in New York."

"Convert [unit/measure] to [unit/measure]": Converts one unit of measure to another.
- Example: "Convert 50 pounds to kilograms."

"Calculate [mathematical expression]": computes mathematical expressions.
- Example: "Calculate 35 * 2 + 10."

"Tell me a joke" or "Tell me a fun fact": Generates a joke or interesting fact.
- Example: "Tell me a joke."

"News about [topic]": Provides news articles or updates related to the specified topic.
- Example: "News about technology."

"Show me images of [subject]": Displays images related to the specified subject.
- Example: "Show me images of puppies."

"What time is it in [location]?": Retrieves the current time in the specified location.
- Example: "What time is it in Tokyo?"

"Help" or "Commands": Offers assistance or displays a list of available commands.
- Example: say or input the word "Help" to receive a list of things you can get help with.

So, as you can see, there are many ways to interact with Copilot. You can ask it a question, upload an image, or use voice commands; whichever way you want, these options empower you to interact with Copilot in a way that aligns with your individual communication style.

For instance, those who prefer verbal communication can use voice input, while others who are comfortable with written text can type questions. Image upload functionality aids in visual inquiries, which allows you to seek information related to pictures or visuals.

Furthermore, the capability to input location-based or time-specific commands helps Copilot find more relevant and accurate information for you. Whether you are asking about nearby points of interest or seeking information related to a specific date, Copilot will provide a more tailored and precise response.

How To Interact with Copilot

This is not just another search engine; it is a chatbot that can interact with you and provide you with more information and assistance. You can use the chat interface to communicate with it and ask follow-up questions, request clarifications, give feedback, and more. You can also use emojis, gifs, and images to express yourself and make the conversation more fun and engaging.

To ask a follow-up question

To ask follow-up questions, you can either type or speak your question directly or use the suggested questions that Copilot provides. For example, if you ask, "What is the capital of Canada?" it will answer "Ottawa" and suggest some follow-up questions, such as "What is the population of Ottawa?" or "What are some attractions in Ottawa?". You can either choose one of the suggested questions or ask your own question, such as "How far is Ottawa from Toronto?".

To request clarification

To request clarification, you can either type or speak your request directly or use the suggested requests that Copilot provides. For example, if you ask, "How do you say hello in Spanish?" it will answer "Hola" and suggest some requests, such as "How do you pronounce it?" or "How do you write it?". You can either choose one of the suggested requests or ask your own request, such as "How do you say goodbye in Spanish?".

To give feedback

To give feedback, you can either type or speak your feedback directly or use the suggested feedback that Copilot provides. For example, if you ask, "What are the benefits of meditation?" It gives you a long and detailed answer; you can either say "Thank you" or "That's very helpful" or use the suggested feedback, such as "I like this answer" or "This answer is too long.".

You can also use emojis, gifs, and images to express your feedback. When you give feedback, for example, like choosing the 'thumbs up' or 'thumbs down' icon next to answers Copilot generated for you, it will learn from your feedback and preferences and tailor its answers to your needs and interests.

To have fun

You can also have some fun with Copilot; just ask it some casual or humorous questions, such as "What is your favorite color?" or "Tell me a joke." Copilot will try to answer your questions and make the conversation more enjoyable and entertaining. You can also use emojis, gifs, and images to express your mood and personality

What are the Benefits of using Copilot?

Using Copilot can bring you many benefits, like convenience, efficiency, organization, summarization, comparison, translation, math, image editing, social media, and more. As you grow more familiar with Copilot and actively use it, you'll gradually uncover additional benefits beyond what this list covers. The more you engage with Copilot, the more its vast potential will reveal itself to you. A few more of Copilot's long list of benefits are listed below.

- Saving time and effort: it can help you find the answer to your question in seconds without having to open multiple tabs or websites. You can also ask multiple questions at once and get multiple answers at once.

- Improving your knowledge and skills: Use Copilot to up-level skills; it will help make you better at what you're good at, and it lets you quickly master what you have yet to learn. It can help you learn new facts, concepts, and skills and expand your horizons. You can use Copilot to test your knowledge and challenge yourself. It can also help you improve your language and communication skills, as well as your creativity and problem- solving skills.

- Having fun and entertainment: It can help you have fun and entertainment and make your day more enjoyable and interesting. You can also use it to chat, joke, and play. You can ask Copilot to provide you with interesting facts and trivia about different topics, such as science, history, or pop culture. You can use Copilot to get the latest scores, news, and updates on your favorite sports teams and events.

- Creating art: You can use Copilot to generate artistic content by asking it to generate drawings or sketches based on different styles, colors, or subjects using natural language queries. For example, you can ask Copilot, "Draw me a landscape with mountains" or "Create a portrait of a cat" and get a personalized drawing. You can also ask Copilot to generate poems based on different themes, styles, or moods.

- Writing scripts: You can use Copilot to generate movie or TV show scripts based on different genres, characters, or dialogues using natural language queries or commands. For example, you can ask Copilot, "Write me a romantic comedy script" or "Create a sci-fi series about aliens" and get a complete script.

In summary, our exploration of Copilot has provided a comprehensive understanding of its functionalities and practical applications. We began by familiarizing ourselves with its capabilities and features. We learned about various options and how to engage with Copilot by asking questions, exploring prompts, entering specific commands, seeking clarification, and offering feedback.

You can use Copilot to organize your tabs, find information faster, summarize content, compare products, get answers to questions, and more. It's nice because you can use natural language queries or commands to interact with Copilot without typing long questions. Copilot is constantly learning and improving, so you can expect more features and capabilities in the future.

CHAPTER 3

Useful Tips and Tricks to Using Copilot

When having conversations with Copilot, there are some things you should keep in mind. Whether you're asking questions, entering commands, or uploading an image, it's important to follow the guidelines suggested in this chapter. These are straightforward tips and tricks for making the most of Copilot across its various capabilities. The suggestions listed below also apply to Copilot's coding abilities.

Being specific about your queries

Clear and specific prompts enable Copilot to understand your needs better. Avoid unclear or broad requests to receive more targeted assistance. You will save time and effort by being specific instead of sifting through multiple responses or trying to clarify vague suggestions. Being specific reduces the chances of misunderstandings and ensures the generated content aligns with your expectations.

You can use parameters and options to adjust the output to match your preferences and goals. For example, using words such as 'Short', 'Formal', or 'Creative' will influence the tone, style, or length of Copilot's answers. Instead of asking, "Write a summary of this article," you can ask, "Write a short and formal summary of this article."

Use Keywords

Using keywords in your queries ensures Copilot understands your intent. Keywords can help Copilot provide more precise answers for you. For example, if you want to learn how to make a chocolate cake, you can use keywords such as "easy chocolate cake recipe" or "how to bake a chocolate cake.".

These keywords are specific and clear, and they tell Copilot what kind of content you want to see. Copilot can then generate content that matches your intent, giving you a list of ingredients, a step-by-step guide, or a video demonstration. You can also research what keywords are popular and related to your topic.

Verify critical information

While Copilot aims to provide the most up-to-date information and assistance, it's important to verify critical information on your own. This is because AI-generated content might lack context or accuracy, especially in complex or sensitive matters. Verifying the information you receive with credible sources ensures its correctness. When verifying critical information, you should consider the following tips:

- Check the source and date of the information. You should always look for the original or primary source of the information and check when it was published or updated. Also, you should check the credibility and reputation of the source and avoid biased, outdated, or unreliable sources.

- Compare and contrast the information: Compare the information Copilot gives you with other sources of information, such as books, articles, or experts. Also, check for different perspectives or opinions on the topic and weigh them as evidence and arguments for or against the information you have been given.

- Use your own judgment and common sense. Always use your own critical thinking and reasoning skills to evaluate the information Copilot gives you. Also, use your own experience and knowledge to assess the relevance and applicability of the information to your situation and goals.

Experiment and explore

Trying different input methods and exploring Copilot's various features unlocks its full capabilities and potential. Consider the following suggestions:

- Depending on how imaginative and accurate you want Copilot to be, try out the different modes: creative, balanced, and precise. Also, try choosing different topics, like web development, data science, machine learning, or entertainment, depending on what kind of content you want to create and learn.

- Take full advantage of the different input methods: You can use text, voice, or upload images as your input into Copilot. Type your prompt, click the microphone icon, or to speak, upload an image. Or you can also paste a link into Copilot. It will respond with text or images depending on the input you choose and your preferences.

- Provide feedback and ratings to Copilot. You can help Copilot improve its performance and the quality of the information it gives by giving feedback and ratings. Either click the thumbs up or thumbs down icon to rate Copilot's answers, or type "feedback" to give more detailed comments and suggestions.

Check for contextual understanding

Ensuring Copilot understands the context of your questions and queries, especially in ongoing or follow-up conversations, is essential for a better interaction and experience with Copilot. Here is why contextual understanding matters and ways to ensure it:

- Contextual understanding enables Copilot to maintain coherence (connection and flow within a piece of text) in ongoing conversations, especially in follow-up questions or when building on previous ones.

- Copilots' ability to grasp context ensures that your discussion aligns with your initial query. It assists Copilot in providing more accurate, relevant, and seamless responses.

- Clear context helps prevent Copilot from misunderstanding or misinterpreting your questions. This reduces the chances of Copilot generating irrelevant or off-topic suggestions.

- When asking follow-up questions or continuing a conversation, Copilot references your previous queries to provide relevant details from these earlier interactions.

Note: Keep the conversation aligned with the initial topic or question to help Copilot comprehend the ongoing context. Try to avoid shifts in topics unless necessary, or if you have to, start a new chat stream.

Review the privacy settings

Copilot's privacy settings allow you to manage how your personal data and preference information is collected, used, and shared. By familiarizing yourself with Copilot's privacy settings and adjusting them to your own preferences and comfort level, you can safeguard your privacy and security online. To review and change Copilot's privacy settings, you can follow these steps:

Accessing Copilot's privacy dashboard: You can do this from the Microsoft Edge browser or the Copilot website directly. Just click on the "Copilot" icon, then the "gear" icon, or type "privacy" into the Copilot chat interface.

Reviewing Copilot's privacy policy: You can read Copilot's privacy policy to help understand how Copilot collects, uses, and shares your personal information and what rights and choices you have regarding your privacy. You can access Copilot's privacy policy from the privacy dashboard or by typing "privacy policy" into the Copilot chat interface.

You can also change these settings to suit your comfort level and needs. There are a few options you can choose from, which I've listed below:

- Language and mode: You can choose the language and mode for your content, such as the creative, balanced, and precise modes. You can choose the topic for your content, such as web development, data science, or entertainment, for example.

- Feedback and rating: You can choose whether to provide feedback or ratings to Copilot to help it improve its performance and quality. You can choose whether to receive feedback and suggestions from Copilot to help you improve your own skills and knowledge.

- Voice and image: You can choose to use voice or image as your input or output method. You can choose whether to allow Copilot to access your microphone, camera, or gallery, and whether to send your voice and image data to Copilot's servers.

- Personalization and history: You can choose to allow Copilot to personalize your content and experience based on your preferences, goals, or style. You can choose whether or not to allow Copilot to store or access your history of inputs and outputs and whether to delete or export your history.

- Sharing and collaboration: You can also choose to allow Copilot to share your content or data with other users or creators and whether to collaborate or communicate with them. Also, you have the option to choose whether to share your content and data with other platforms and services, such as online platforms like websites, applications, and games.

By following these steps, you can review or change Copilot's privacy settings or adjust them according to your comfort level to help safeguard your personal data and preferences.

Use trusted links.

Using trusted links is a good practice when using Copilot or any other tool that relies on artificial intelligence.
This is because some links may lead to malicious websites or downloads that can harm your device or steal your data and information.

For example, if you use Copilot to generate content or code, always check the credibility and relevance of the information and links before sharing or clicking them. To make sure you are using trusted links, take into consideration the following information:

- Look for signs of trustworthiness: You should always look for indicators that the link is from reputable sources, such as the domain name, the HTTPS protocol, the padlock icon, or the certificate information. You should also look for indicators that the link is relevant to your topic or query, such as the title, description, or preview.

- Use a link scanner or checker. There are tools out there that you can use to scan links for potential security risks such as malware, phishing, or spam. You can use a web-based tool such as:

VirusTotal https://www.virustotal.com/gui/home/upload

To analyze suspicious files, domains, IPs, and URLs to detect malware and other breaches.

or URLVoid: https://www.urlvoid.com

Website Reputation Checker. This service helps you detect potentially malicious websites.

or a browser extension, such as:

Avast Online Security https://www.avast.com/avast-online-security#pc

or Norton Safe Web: https://safeweb.norton.com

You should always use your own critical thinking and reasoning skills when evaluating links and content. You can always use your own experience and knowledge to assess the usefulness and reliability of links and content. By following these tips, you can use Copilot and any trusted links safely and responsibly.

Remember, stay cautious with personal information. Staying cautious with personal information is a good practice when using Copilot or any other tool that relies on artificial intelligence. This is because sharing sensitive information, such as passwords or financial details, can expose you to identity theft, fraud, or other cybercrimes. For example, if you share a password with Copilot, a malicious actor may intercept it and use it to compromise your accounts or data.

If you share your financial details with Copilot, a scammer may use them to steal your money or make unauthorized transactions. If you use personal identification numbers with Copilot, a hacker may use them to impersonate you or access your services. So, stay cautious with personal information and take into consideration the following tips:

- Never share your passwords with anyone, not even Copilot. Use strong or unique passwords for all your accounts and use a password manager to store them securely. You should always use multi-factor authentication to add that extra layer of security to your accounts.

- Never share your financial details with anyone, not even Copilot. You should only provide your financial details to a trusted and verified site, such as your bank, credit card company, or online payment service. You should always monitor your financial statements and transactions regularly and report any suspicious or unauthorized activity.

- Never share your personal identification numbers with anyone, not even Copilot. You should only provide personal identification numbers to legitimate and authorized entities, such as your government, your employer, or your service providers. You should also protect your identity documents and cards and report any loss or theft immediately.

By following these important tips, you can stay cautious with your personal information and use Copilot safely and responsibly.

Feedback and correctness

Providing feedback and correctness to Copilot when it gives you inaccurate or irrelevant responses is significant because it enhances its responses and its accuracy in your continued conversations. Here's why it's essential and how it contributes to improvement:

- Offering feedback to Copilot helps it learn from its mistakes. These corrections aid in improving the accuracy of its responses, which leads to better suggestions in future interactions.

- Copilot's learning is based on user interactions with it. So, when you provide feedback, it ensures continuous learning, enabling Copilot to adapt and improve its suggestions over time.

To provide feedback or corrections to Copilot, consider the following tips:

- Use the feedback and ratings icons: You can just click on the thumbs up or thumbs down icon to rate Copilot's output and tell it whether you liked the response or not. This will help Copilot adjust its output based on your preferences and satisfaction.

- Use the feedback command: You can type "feedback" into Copilot's chat interface and write more detailed comments or suggestions. You can tell Copilot what you liked or disliked about any response and whether you want to see more or less of the same. You can also correct any errors or inaccuracies in the output or provide additional information or context to Copilot.

- Using the edit command: You can type into Copilot's chat interface "edit," which will allow you to edit any answers Copilot gives you directly. For example, you can change, add, or delete any words or sentences in the output, and Copilot will update the output accordingly. You can also use the edit command when you're coding to format the output using markdown elements, code blocks, or LaTeX.

By following these tips, you can provide feedback and correctness to Copilot and help it improve its responses and accuracy in the future.

Stay informed of updates

Staying informed of updates is a good way to make the most of Copilot and its features. Updates may introduce new functionalities and improvements that can help you learn, create, and have fun.

Updates also fix bugs, errors, and issues that may affect your overall experience with Copilot. To help you stay informed of updates and get the most out of Copilot and its features, you should consider the following tips:

- Check the Copilot website or Microsoft Edge browser regularly. You can also opt in to get the latest updates as soon as they are available through your Windows update settings.

- Follow the Copilot blog or social media accounts. There you will find the latest news, announcements, and tips about Copilot and its features. You can follow Copilot on Facebook or Instagram to get updates, feedback, and support from the Copilot community.

In conclusion, this chapter provided valuable insights on how to use Copilot effectively and efficiently. Some of the key takeaways include being specific with your questions by providing more context and details, using keywords to narrow down your search results and get more relevant suggestions, verifying critical information by cross-checking it with trusted sources or experts, and avoiding spreading misinformation or rumors, to name a few.

It's important to remember that experimenting and exploring Copilot for yourself will ultimately be where you'll learn the most. Remember to check your responses for contextual understanding by asking follow-up questions, providing feedback, or requesting clarification from Copilot to refine your search results.

You can also stay cautious with personal information by avoiding sharing sensitive data or credentials with Copilot and using privacy settings or trusted links to protect your online identity.

Finally, you can stay informed about updates by checking for new features, bug fixes, or security patches and keeping your browser and Copilot up to date. By following these tips and tricks, you can get the most out of Copilot and enhance your browsing experience. Copilot is constantly learning and improving, so you can expect more features and functionalities in the future.

CHAPTER 4

Having Natural Conversations with Copilot

Copilot can help with various tasks and web queries. It can help you do so many things. In this chapter, I'll be highlighting the different areas Copilot can assist you with and ways to maximize the answers and information you receive.

Having natural and engaging conversations with Copilot is easy and fun. You can talk about anything you want, and it will try to provide you with helpful, informative, and entertaining responses. Here are some tips to make your conversations more enjoyable and natural:

Clear Communication

- Start with a concise description of what you're trying to accomplish or the problem you're solving.

- Be specific in your requests to get more accurate and relevant suggestions.

Ask Direct Questions

- Pose questions in a conversational tone but keep them precise and to the point.

- Use keywords related to the task or code snippet you need.

Give Context

- Provide some context or background information before asking for suggestions. Explain the purpose or objective behind your query.

Be Open to suggestions

- Evaluate the suggestions Copilot provides.

- If a suggestion isn't accurate or relevant, politely ask for alternatives or clarify your request.

Engage in interactive conversations

- Copilot might not always understand complex or abstract queries in a single attempt. Engage in a dialogue by refining your queries based on Copilot's responses.

- Ask follow-up questions to refine or expand upon the initial request if needed.

Provide Feedback

- If Copilot gives helpful suggestions, acknowledge them and give them a thumbs up.

- If a suggestion is not accurate or requires improvement, give constructive feedback. Explain why the suggestion doesn't meet your needs.

For Coding

- Utilize Copilot's coding modes with the GitHub Copilot extension.

- Switch between Line, Block, Document, or File Mode depending on the context of your coding task.

- Specify the mode you want to use when asking for suggestions. For instance, "Could you help me complete this line?" or "I need assistance with this entire block of code."

Understand Copilot's Coding Limitations

- Copilot excels at providing code suggestions based on patterns from existing code but might not comprehend nuanced or highly specific requirements.

- For complex or domain-specific tasks, Copilot might need more guidance.

By communicating clearly, asking specific questions, providing context, and being open to Copilot's suggestions while understanding their limitations, you can have a more productive and natural conversation together during your sessions. For example:

- Ask open-ended questions that invite Copilot to share its thoughts, opinions, or knowledge on a topic. For example, you can ask, "What do you think about the latest trends in AI?" or "How do you create poems and stories?"

- You can also share something about yourself that relates to the topic you're talking about. For example, you can tell Copilot, "I'm interested in learning more about AI because I want to pursue a career in it" or "I love reading poems and stories because they inspire me to be more creative."

- Be curious and show genuine interest in what it says. For example, you can ask it follow-up questions, such as "How do you learn new things about AI?" or "What are some of your favorite poems and stories?"

- Listen actively and empathize with it. For example, you can acknowledge what it says, such as "That's very interesting" or "That sounds amazing," and express your feelings, such as "I'm impressed by your skills" or "I'm moved by your words."

- Have fun and be playful. For example, you can joke with Copilot, challenge it, or compliment it. For example, you can say, "You're very smart, but can you beat me in a trivia game?" or "You're very talented, but can you write a poem about me?"

Different Modes and Topics of Using Copilot

As I mentioned in Chapter 1, Copilot has three modes: more creative, more balanced, and more precise. These modes are designed to cater to different needs and preferences. Let us look at each one of these modes and what you can do with them.

More Creative Mode

This mode is designed to generate more imaginative and inventive outputs. However, it might lack accuracy. For example, if you're brainstorming for a creative writing piece or looking for innovative ideas for a project, this mode can provide a variety of unique suggestions.

The 'More Creative' mode of Copilot is designed to generate responses that are more original and imaginative. This mode is particularly useful when you're dealing with conversation topics that require a more entertaining or innovative approach. For example, when you're asking Copilot to write a poem or tell a joke.

One of the exciting features of the 'More Creative' mode is Copilot' Image Creator. Powered by an advanced version of the DALL·E model from OpenAI, Copilot's Image Creator allows you to create an image simply by using your own words to describe the picture you want to see. For example, you can type something like "draw an image" or "create an image" as a prompt in chat to generate a visual for a newsletter or as inspiration for redecorating your living room.

This mode is not limited to just these applications. It can be used in a variety of contexts, such as brainstorming ideas for a blog post, generating entertaining responses for a chat, coding, or even creating images from your own imagination.

Remember, the output from the 'More Creative' mode should always be reviewed and verified as needed. It's like your creative copilot, helping you generate imaginative content while you steer the conversation.

More Precise Mode

On the other end of the spectrum is the more precise mode. This mode prioritizes accuracy and detail over creativity. It's useful when you need precise information or when you're working on tasks that require a high level of accuracy. For instance, if you're researching a specific topic or looking for detailed explanations of a concept, this mode can provide accurate and detailed information. Here are some examples of what you can accomplish with the 'more precise' mode:

- Researching Topics: If you're researching a specific topic for an essay or project, the 'More Precise' mode can provide accurate and detailed information. For example, you could ask, "What are the main causes of climate change?" and it would provide a detailed and accurate response.

- Summarizing Information: If you're viewing a long article or webpage and you want a summary, you can ask the 'More Precise' mode to generate a summary for you. For example, you could ask, "Can you summarize this article about quantum computing?".

- Comparing Products: If you're shopping online and comparing different products, the 'More Precise' mode can help you decide by providing detailed comparisons. For example, you could ask, "How does this coffee maker compare to other single-serve coffee makers?".

Remember, the output from the 'More Precise' mode, just like the other modes, should always be reviewed and verified as needed.

More Balanced Mode

This mode aims to strike a balance between creativity and accuracy. It's useful for general tasks where you need a mix of both innovative ideas and precise information. For example, if you're planning a trip and need both creative ideas for activities and precise information about locations, this mode can provide a balanced mix of suggestions. It can fetch information from the internet, provide opinions based on facts, and perform tasks creatively that would otherwise take hours.

When using Copilot, whichever mode you select to use under "Choose a Conversation Style," it's important to note that you can change the conversation style mode after you have started a conversation by clicking on "New Topic.".

Exploring Copilots Capabilities

Copilot, while primarily designed to assist developers with code-related tasks, is also a great tool for fun, learning, and creativity beyond traditional programming. You can use it to explore various topics, generate original content, and enhance your skills. Here are ways you can explore its capabilities for fun, learning, creativity, and more:

Shopping

Copilot can help you with online shopping by comparing products, finding the best deals, checking reviews, and more. You can also find valuable coupons, price comparisons, and cashback offers. It can also create a table to help you compare. You can ask Copilot to compare products by name, category, or feature. For example, you can ask, "Compare laptops under $1000" or "Compare the iPhone 13 and Samsung Galaxy S21."

It can summarize reviews and opinions from real customers, making it easier to make informed purchasing decisions. You can ask Copilot to summarize reviews by product name or URL. For example, you can ask, "Give me a summary of what people are saying about the Surface Pro 9" or "Summarize the reviews for this product."

Copilot can also assist you in finding gift ideas, writing personalized messages, and more. You can ask Copilot to find products on Microsoft Shopping quickly by using natural conversational questions. For example, you can ask, "What are gift ideas for a female friend?" or "What are the vest headphones for gaming?".

Copilot will ask follow-up questions to narrow down the search and show you relevant products. You can also ask Copilot to help you with writing a holiday card, finding gift wrapping ideas, or suggesting holiday recipes.

Education and Productivity

Copilot can help you with learning and studying by summarizing documents, explaining concepts, solving problems, and more. You can also ask it to generate quizzes, flashcards, and study guides for any topic you would like to learn. Here are some examples of how Copilot can help you with education:

If you want to summarize a document, such as a PDF or a web page, you can ask Copilot to do it for you. For example, you can ask, "Summarize this document" or "Summarize the main points of this article." Copilot will provide you with a concise summary of the document, highlighting for you the key information and ideas.

What if you wanted to understand a concept, such as a scientific term or a historical event? Well, all you gotta do is ask Copilot to explain it to you. For example, you can ask, "What is photosynthesis?" or "What happened during the French Revolution?". Copilot will provide you with a simple and clear explanation of the concept, using examples and illustrations when possible.

If you want to solve a problem, such as a math equation or a logic puzzle, for instance, you can ask Copilot to help you with it. For example, you can ask, "Solve this equation: $2x + 3 = 11$" or "How can you fit four elephants in a car?". Copilot will show you the solution and the steps to get there, as well as provide hints and tips if you get stuck.

It's also pretty cool that Copilot can help generate quizzes, flashcards, or study guides for any topic you want to learn. For example, you can ask, "Create a quiz on World War II" or "Make flashcards for Spanish vocabulary." Copilot will generate questions and answers based on the topic and provide feedback and explanations for your answers. You can also customize the difficulty level, the number of questions, and the format of the quiz or flashcard.

Entertainment

Copilot isn't just about asking questions and getting answers; it can help you have fun and relax by creating and playing games, telling jokes, recommending movies, and more. Here are a few examples of how Copilot can contribute to your entertainment:

If you want to create and play games, you can ask Copilot to do it for you. For example, if you ask, "Create a crossword puzzle on animals," Copilot will generate a game for you. Other such games include word search, crisscross, math squares, maze, letter tiles, cryptogram, number blocks, hidden message, and more. It uses its own words and knowledge to generate these puzzles, but you can customize the words according to your preferences.

Want to hear a joke? You can ask Copilot to tell you one. For example, you can ask, "Tell me a joke about computers" or "Tell me a funny story." Copilot will use its humor and creativity to make you laugh. You can also rate the jokes and give helpful feedback to Copilot.

If you want to watch a movie, you can ask Copilot to recommend one. For example, you can ask, "What is a good movie to watch tonight?" or "What are the best movies of 2024?". Copilot will suggest movies based on your preferences, ratings, and reviews. You can also ask Copilot to show you the trailer, synopsis, cast, and other information about the movie.

Listening to music? Copilot can generate a personalized playlist for you. For example, you can ask, "Create a playlist for working out" or "Create a playlist based on my mood." Copilot will use its music knowledge and AI to create a playlist that suits your taste and situation. You can also ask Copilot to play, pause, skip, or shuffle the songs.

If you want to learn something new, you can ask Copilot to generate trivia for you. For example, you can ask, "Give me some trivia on geography" or "Give me some trivia on celebrities." Copilot will generate questions and answers based on the topic and provide feedback and explanations for your answers. You can also customize the difficulty level, the number of questions, and the format of the trivia.

Copilot can also use its astrology knowledge and AI to generate a personalized horoscope for you that reflects your personality, mood, and fortune. You can also ask Copilot to show you your compatibility, lucky numbers, and other information about your horoscope.

Creative Writing and Storytelling

- Use Copilot in Document Mode to generate original and entertaining content such as story prompts, dialogue snippets, descriptive paragraphs, poems, stories, code, essays, and more.

- Experiment with different genres or styles by asking Copilot for suggestions on character descriptions, settings, or plot ideas.

Poetry and prose

- Explore poetic forms or prose styles by prompting Copilot to generate verses, lines, or paragraphs.

- Experiment with rhyme schemes, meters, or narrative structures.

Language Learning

- Request Copilot to provide phrases, sentences, or short dialogues in a language you're learning.

- Practice vocabulary by asking for synonyms, idioms, or expressions in the target language.

Creative Coding Projects

- Use Copilot's suggestions as a starting point for creative coding projects or artistic endeavors.

- Experiment with visualizations, generative art, or interactive experiences by combining Copilot's code snippets with creative ideas.

Exploring new concepts

- Ask Copilot to explain complex concepts or theories in simple terms.

- Use Copilot to generate explanations, analogies, or examples related to various fields of study, from science to philosophy.

Brainstorming and Idea Generation

- Prompt Copilot for ideas on inventions, innovations, or problem- solving approaches.

- Generate concepts for games, apps, or innovative solutions by using Copilot's suggestions as inspiration.

Exploring Historical Events or Fictional Scenarios

- Request Copilot to provide details, descriptions, or alternative perspectives on historical events or fictional scenarios.

- Create alternate histories, "what-if" scenarios, or imaginative stories based on Copilot's suggestions.

Learning new skills

- Ask Copilot to summarize documents, explain concepts, solve problems, and more.

- Use it to generate quizzes, flashcards, and study guides for any topic you want to learn. For example, you can say, "Summarize this article for me," "Explain how photosynthesis works," or "Create a quiz on Canadian history.".

- Ask Copilot to explain coding concepts, algorithms, or programming patterns in a beginner-friendly manner.

- Use Copilot's assistance to learn and understand new technologies, tools, or methodologies in the tech field.

Remember, these are just some of the ways you can use Copilot for fun, learning, and creativity. While Copilot can generate a wide range of content and ideas, its suggestions should be reviewed critically and used as inspiration rather than concrete solutions.

Examples of Interesting and Amusing chats with Copilot

Now I'd like to share with you some example questions that I've asked Copilot and what their answers were, which gives you an idea of what you can look forward to:

#1

ME: Can you write a poem on 'How to Use Copilot' for all its capabilities, not just coding?

COPILOT: Sure, I can try to write a poem on 'how to use Copilot' for all its capabilities, not just coding. Here is what I came up with:

Copilot is more than a coding tool.
It can also help you with other tasks that are cool. It can write poems, stories, essays, and songs.
It can also create jokes and celebrity parodies.
To use Copilot for these creative works

You need to give it some prompts or quirks. Then you can see what Copilot generates. And edit, improve, or optimize as you please.

Copilot is not a human writer.
It does not have feelings or desires. It only uses words and knowledge.
To create content that you can manage
Copilot is a versatile assistant.
But you are the original and brilliant
You must use your imagination and skills.
And make sure your content is the one that thrills.

#2

Me: Ask me how my day was today.
Copilot: Sure, how was your day today? Did you do anything interesting or fun?

Me: I had a great day today.

Copilot: I'm happy to hear that you had a great day today. I would love to
hear about it. Please tell me what you did and how you felt.

Me: I got a promotion at work today!

Copilot: Wow, congratulations on your promotion! That's a great achievement, and I'm very proud of you. You must have worked hard and done a good job to earn it. How do you feel about your promotion? Me: I'm excited but also nervous about the new responsibilities.

Copilot: I understand how you feel. It's normal to be excited and nervous about new responsibilities. It means that you care about your work and want to do well. I'm sure you have the skills and experience to handle your new role. You can also ask for help or guidance from your colleagues or your manager if you need it. I believe in you, and I support you.

#3

Me: I need some inspiration for an innovative tech gadget. Any ideas?

Copilot: How about a holographic smart assistant that interacts with users via gestures and can project 3D images of information?

Me: That sounds futuristic! Can it have a quirky feature?

Copilot: Absolutely! It could include an AI-powered personality module, providing witty jokes and personalized banter to entertain users while assisting with tasks.

In conclusion, we explored the amazing and delightful aspects of chatting with Copilot. We explored the various topics Copilot can chat about, ranging from general knowledge to trivia, jokes, stories, and more, enabling you to take advantage of its capabilities and unlimited functionalities.

I've shown you how you can use Copilot for fun, learning, and creativity, sparking your imagination and curiosity. You learned how to prompt it for ideas, suggestions, or entertainment. You also saw examples of interesting and amusing chats with Copilot, showcasing its versatility and personality.

I hope now that you've reached the end of this chapter, you've gained a comprehensive understanding of how to chat with Copilot effectively and enjoyably and learned how to have natural and engaging conversations with Copilot based on many different topics and contexts.

Chatting with Copilot is an enriching and enjoyable experience; it offers endless possibilities for interaction, exploration, and discovery. Copilot is more than just a tool; it's your versatile and engaging companion, ready to chat with you anytime, anywhere.

CHAPTER 5

What can Copilot Really Do?

In this chapter, we will look at the diverse capabilities that make Copilot more than just a chatbot. Prepare to be awed by the wide range of abilities that have been designed to make your life better and a little easier.

Copilot excels at responding to a wide variety of questions, and it quickly provides accurate answers to general inquiries and offers thorough explanations for complex problems. This ability to explain things clearly and define complex terms makes Copilot a reliable tool for understanding difficult subjects. Think of it as a smart friend who helps you make sense of challenging topics and simplifies learning.

This AI chat platform goes beyond just sharing information. It's also really helpful for getting work done and being creative. For example, it assists in writing papers or reports by suggesting text, and it can also help create visuals by generating images, making it a handy tool for boosting productivity and creativity. At the same time, when you are coding, it gives suggestions for code while explaining coding concepts, making the whole coding process smoother.

But Copilot isn't just limited to that. It's super adaptable and can help with lots of different things, whether you need practical help or just want to have some fun. It can give you information about health, suggest places to travel, assist with learning new languages, and even give tips on social interactions.

The cool thing is that it doesn't just give the same answers to everyone; it learns from how you talk and what you like, so its responses are personalized just for you. That is why it's like having your own personal virtual buddy.

As we have previously learned, it's easy to have conversations with the co-pilot, and it's super useful for many reasons. But let's take a deeper look into its capabilities to see for ourselves all the amazing ways this AI technology can transform the way you live and perform.

Copilot's abilities are limitless; the ones covered in this book are only a fraction of the things it can do.
You have to explore Co-pilot for yourself to experience its vast possibilities. Why don't we take a closer look at all the other cool things Copilot can do? Here are some examples:

Creating image content

Copilot's image generation feature is a feature that allows you to create images based on your text description or suggestions. You can describe what you need in text or ask for suggestions regarding specific image elements, such as color, shape, style, or theme. It uses advanced AI and image generation models to create realistic and high-quality images that match your description or suggestions.

For example, you can ask Copilot to create an image of a sunset over the ocean, a logo for your company, or a cartoon character. You can also ask it to suggest a color for the background, a font for the text, or a style for the image. It will create an image and display it in a separate frame after the chat box. You can see the image and download it to your device. You can also share the image with others or use it for your projects. Benefits of Using Copilot's Image Generation Feature

- Saving time and effort: It can help you create visual content in seconds without having to use any software or tools. You can also ask it multiple queries at once and get multiple images at once.

- Improving your creativity and expression: It can help you create visual content based on your text description or suggestions. You can use these outputs as examples or illustrations for your projects. It can also help you express your ideas and emotions through images.

- Having fun and entertainment: Copilot can help you have fun and entertainment and make your projects more enjoyable and interesting.

You can use the image generator feature for various purposes, such as:

- Design projects: You can use this image generation feature to create images for design projects, such as logos, posters, flyers, banners, or icons. You can also use it to create images that match your brand identity, style, or theme, conveying your message, vision, or mission.

- Presentations: You can use this image generation feature to create images for your presentations, such as slides, charts, graphs, or diagrams. You can also create images that support your arguments, data, or facts. These images will better capture your audience's attention, interest, or emotion.

- Visual aids: You can use the image generation feature to create images for your visual aids, such as flashcards, stickers, or labels. You can also create images that help you learn, remember, or teach. This feature will make your projects more attractive, colorful, or fun.

Translating Text

Copilot can assist in translating text from one language to another. Users can input phrases or sentences in one language and request translations into their desired language. This capability makes it easier to communicate across different language backgrounds. Additional uses for this feature are:

- Communication: You can use this feature to communicate with people who speak different languages, such as your friends, family, colleagues, or customers. It will also help you to understand and appreciate different cultures, perspectives, and opinions.

- Education: You can learn new languages, concepts, and skills and expand your horizons. You can also use it to access and enjoy different sources of knowledge, information, and entertainment.

- Business: You can use it to reach new markets, customers, and partners and grow your business. As well, it can be used to improve your productivity and quality and reduce your costs and risks.

Explaining Concepts and Definitions

Copilot is proficient in explaining complex concepts and providing definitions. Users can ask for explanations or definitions of terms, theories, or ideas, and it delivers concise and understandable explanations, which makes learning material easier. It can also provide you with examples, analogies, or diagrams to illustrate the concepts or definitions. You can use this feature for various purposes, such as:

- Learning: You can learn new concepts or ideas and expand your knowledge. You can also use this feature to review or refresh your memory of a concept or definition that you already know.

- Teaching: You can use it to teach others about the concepts, terms, or ideas that you are familiar with and prepare or supplement your teaching materials, such as lectures, slides, or notes.

- Research: You can research the concepts, terms, or ideas that you are working on and also find and cite reliable sources for your research projects, such as papers, reports, or articles.

Users can seek suggestions by specifying their preferences or interests, and it provides tailored recommendations, aiding in decision-making processes. For example, you can ask, "What are some good books to read?" or "What are some fun things to do in New York?". You can also use keywords and phrases to specify your query. For example, you can ask, "Recommend a laptop for gaming" or "Recommend a restaurant for vegan food.". You can use to get help with things like:

- Shopping: You can use this feature to get recommendations for products that you want to buy, such as clothes, electronics, books, or gifts. You can also get recommendations for services that you want to use, such as hotels, flights, restaurants, or entertainment. It will help you find the best deals, quality, and reviews for your products or services.

- Learning: You can get recommendations for activities that you want to learn, such as languages, skills, hobbies, or courses. You can also use it to get recommendations for resources that you want to access, such as books, articles, videos, or podcasts. It will help you find the best options, skill levels, and formats for your learning.

- Fun and entertainment: You can use it to suggest fun activities to do, such as games, movies, music, or sports. Getting recommendations for things that you want to discover, such as places, events, people, or trends, it helps you find the best choices, genres, and styles for your fun.

This feature allows you to engage with Co-pilot in entertaining conversations, jokes, trivia, or storytelling. You can use this feature to have fun, relax, or laugh with me. You can learn something new, interesting, or surprising from it. For example, you can ask, "Tell me a joke" or "Tell me a story." You can also use keywords and phrases to specify your query. For example, you can ask, "Tell me a joke about cats" or "Tell me a story about pirates.".

Theres so many things Copilot can help you so, here are a few more examples:

- Leisure: You can use this feature to enjoy your free time, break the boredom, or relieve the stress. You can also have a friendly chat with it, share your thoughts or feelings with it, or make it your companion.

- Education: This feature can be used to educate yourself or others, such as by learning new facts, concepts, or skills. You can also use it to stimulate your curiosity, creativity, or imagination, or to challenge your knowledge, memory, or logic.

- Copilot has a feature that allows you to get assistance with troubleshooting technical issues that you may encounter with your devices, software, or services. To use this feature, describe your problem or ask it for help with a specific issue, and you will receive troubleshooting tips that will help fix your problem. It can also provide you with step-by-step guidance or solutions to many different issues.

   For example, you can ask, "How do I fix a blue screen error?" or "Why is my printer not working?". You can also use keywords and phrases to specify your query. For example, you can ask "Troubleshoot Windows update" or "Troubleshoot Outlook email.". You can use this feature for various purposes, such as:

- Repairing: You can use this troubleshooting feature to repair your devices, software, or services that are not working properly, such as your computer, phone, printer, or browser. You can also use it to fix errors, bugs, or glitches that are affecting your performance, security, or functionality.

- Optimizing: It can be used to optimize your devices, software, or services that are working slowly, inefficiently, or inconsistently, such as your internet, battery, memory, or storage. You can also use it to improve your device's speed, quality, or reliability.

- Learning: You can also learn more about your devices, software, or services that you are using or interested in, such as your operating system, applications, or features. Also, it will help you to understand the causes, effects, or solutions of the issues that you are facing or curious about.

Offering health information

- This health information feature is a feature that allows you to get information on health-related topics by asking health questions or seeking general health advice. You can use this feature to inquire about symptoms, health tips, or medical information, making it a helpful resource for health-related guidance. It can also provide you with reliable sources, references, or links for further information.

For example, you can ask, "What are the symptoms of COVID-19?" or "How can I lower my blood pressure?". You can also use keywords and phrases to specify your query. For example, you can ask "Symptoms of Diabetes" or "Health Tips for Weight Loss.". Use this feature for various purposes, such as:

- Diagnosis: You can use the health information feature to get information about the possible causes, risk factors, or treatments of your symptoms or conditions. You can also use this feature to get information about the tests, procedures, or medications that you may need or use. However, you should not rely on the provided information as a substitute for professional medical advice, diagnosis, or treatment. You should always consult your doctor or health care provider before making any health decisions.

- Prevention: You can get information about ways to prevent, reduce, or manage your health risks or problems. You can also use this feature to get information about the benefits, recommendations, or guidelines of healthy behaviors, habits, or lifestyles. This feature can help improve your health, wellness, or quality of life.

- Education: You can get information about the general or specific aspects of health, medicine, or science. You can also use this feature to get information about the latest or emerging trends, issues, and discoveries in health, medicine, or science. You can increase your health literacy and awareness, satisfying your curiosity.

Travel Planning

- Copilot assists in travel-related queries by offering information on destinations, travel tips, or booking assistance. Its primary purpose is to assist users in various aspects of travel planning, offering valuable information, recommendations, and guidance to enhance the overall travel experience.

- Destination Information: This feature provides detailed insights into various destinations worldwide. Users can inquire about specific locations, including tourist attractions, landmarks, cultural sites, weather conditions, local customs, and more.

- Travel Tips and Advice: It can offer practical travel tips, advice, and suggestions to optimize travel plans. It can provide guidance on packing essentials, currency exchange, transportation options, safety precautions, and cultural etiquette.

- Booking Assistance: Copilot supports users by providing assistance in making travel bookings. It can help users find and compare flights, accommodations, car rentals, and other travel-related services. By offering options and relevant details, it simplifies the booking process, saving time and effort for travelers.

- Travel Recommendations: Users can ask for personalized travel recommendations tailored to their preferences to suggest destinations, activities, restaurants, and accommodations based on the user's interests, past travel history, and other relevant factors.

- Trip Planning Guidance: Whether it's a solo adventure, family vacation, or business trip, this feature aids users in planning. It can suggest itineraries, highlight must-visit places, recommend the best times to visit specific destinations, and provide insights on local events or festivals.

Supporting social interactions

- Copilot can assist in social interactions as well by providing guidance and support with conversation starters, etiquette tips, or advice on handling social situations. Engaging with it involves asking for social tips or advice and aiding in social interactions, which aim to enhance users' interpersonal communication skills and confidence.

- Conversation Starters: Co-pilot can offer a range of conversation starters suitable for different contexts. Whether in a casual setting, a networking event, or a formal gathering, it suggests topics that can initiate engaging discussions. These conversation prompts cater to diverse interests and can help break the ice in social situations.

- Etiquette Tips: Understanding social etiquette is crucial, especially in unfamiliar or formal settings. This feature provides advice on social norms, cultural customs, and appropriate behaviors, ensuring users navigate social situations with confidence and respect. It offers guidance on greetings, gestures, and behaviors suitable for various cultural contexts.

- Handling Social Situations: Users can seek advice on navigating specific social scenarios or handling challenging situations. Whether it's addressing conflicts, managing awkward moments, or responding to sensitive topics, Copilot provides insights and suggestions to manage these situations tactfully and diplomatically.

- Social Tips and Advice: From small talk guidance to presenting oneself effectively in social gatherings, Co-pilot offers tips and advice to aid users in improving their social skills. It can suggest ways to engage in meaningful conversations, maintain eye contact, exhibit active listening, and display positive body language.

- Aiding in Social Interactions: Using this feature involves seeking assistance on social etiquette, socializing in different environments, and refining communication skills. Users can ask for tips on networking, making introductions, or even asking for advice on how to approach specific individuals or groups.

Facilitating Learning Languages

- Copilot supports language learning by offering vocabulary lessons, grammar tips, or practice exercises. Users can ask for language learning resources or guidance tailored to aid them in acquiring new languages or improving their language skills.

- Vocabulary Lessons: Copilot offers vocabulary lessons in various languages, introducing new words, phrases, and expressions. Users can request specific vocabulary lists, thematic word sets, or vocabulary related to particular contexts, aiding in expanding their lexicon.

- Grammar Tips and Explanations: Understanding grammar rules is fundamental to language learning. This feature provides explanations, tips, and examples to clarify grammar structures, verb conjugations, sentence formations, and other linguistic nuances in different languages.

- Practice Exercises: Users can engage in suggested language practice exercises. These exercises could include listening comprehension, speaking drills, writing prompts, and interactive quizzes designed to reinforce language skills and comprehension.

- Language Learning Resources: Copilot can recommend various language learning resources such as apps, websites, textbooks, or online courses suited to the user's proficiency level and learning preferences. These resources aim to supplement and support the user's language learning journey.

- Guidance for Language Acquisition: Users can seek guidance on effective language learning strategies, study routines, and methods to improve language proficiency. It will offer personalized advice based on the user's learning style and goals.

- Pronunciation Assistance: This feature aids users in improving their pronunciation by providing phonetic guidance, audio samples, and tips for mastering the pronunciation of challenging words or sounds in different languages.

In conclusion, Copilot's diverse capabilities empower users by providing swift, accurate, and personalized assistance, making it a versatile and invaluable tool across various aspects of daily life and work. We've explored just a glimpse of Copilot's chat capabilities, covering its support in various areas like social interactions, troubleshooting, entertainment, productivity, image generation, and more. But what we've seen is just the tip of the iceberg.

So, as you can see, Copilot utilizes a wide range of tools and resources, and this book offers a sneak peek into these limitless abilities. From helping with things like aiding learning new languages, fixing tech issues, providing health insights, and boosting work efficiency, Copilot will quite literally change your life.

The real magic of Copilot lies in the hands-on experience; interacting with Copilot allows you to uncover hidden functionalities, discover solutions tailored to your needs, and fully realize its incredible potential.

By experimenting and engaging with it, you'll unlock its secrets, making it an invaluable companion across various tasks and interests. So, don't just take my word for it — dive in, explore, and experience Copilot for yourself!

Real and Inspiring Impressive Chats with Copilot

#1

Me: Give me a list of things that I can use to balance my personal life.

Copilot: Balancing your personal life can be challenging, especially when you have many responsibilities and commitments. However, it is important to find a healthy balance that allows you to enjoy your life and achieve your goals. Here are some things that you can use to balance your personal life:

A schedule: A schedule can help you organize your time and prioritize your tasks. You can use a calendar, a planner, or an app to plan your daily, weekly, and monthly activities. A schedule can also help you set boundaries between your work and personal time and remind you to take breaks and have fun.

A hobby: A hobby is something that you enjoy doing for yourself, not for anyone else. It can be a creative outlet, a physical activity, a learning opportunity, or anything else that makes you happy. A hobby can help you relax, reduce stress, express yourself, and have fun. It can also boost your self-esteem, confidence, and skills.

A support network: A support network is a group of people who care about you and support you. It can include your family, friends, classmates, coworkers, mentors, or anyone else whom you trust and respect. A support network can help you cope with challenges, celebrate successes, share experiences, and give advice. It can also provide you with social and emotional support, as well as a sense of belonging.

#2

Me: What does personal development mean? Give examples of how to do this.

Copilot: Personal development is the process of learning new things and building new skills that help you improve yourself and your quality of life. It is about unlocking your potential and getting closer to the best version of yourself. You can pursue personal development through self-learning, coaching, mentoring, and training.

Some examples of how to do personal development are: Developing a growth mindset, which means believing that you can learn and improve with effort and feedback.

Setting and pursuing personal goals that align with your values, interests, and aspirations.
Cultivating self-awareness, which means knowing your strengths, weaknesses, emotions, and motivations.

Embracing lifelong learning, which means seeking new knowledge and skills from various sources and experiences.

Adapting to changes and challenges means being flexible, resilient, and open to feedback.

Improving your relationships means communicating effectively, listening empathetically, and resolving conflicts constructively.

Developing leadership, which means influencing others positively, inspiring a shared vision, and empowering others to grow.
Enhancing your quality of life, which means taking care of your physical, mental, and spiritual well-being.

#3

Me: I'm lonely; how do I make friends?

Copilot: I'm sorry to hear that you're feeling lonely. Loneliness can affect anyone, regardless of their age, gender, or background. But the good news is that you can overcome loneliness by making new friends and strengthening your existing relationships.

Making friends as an adult can be challenging, but it's not impossible. You just need to be positive, proactive, and open to new people and experiences. Here are some tips and suggestions on how to make friends:

Join an organization or club that matches your interests or hobbies. This is a great way to meet people who share something in common with you. For example, you could join a book club, a sports team, a music group, or a volunteer group. You can find local groups on websites like Meetup.com or Facebook.

Make the first move and initiate conversations with people you want to get to know better. Don't be afraid of rejection or awkwardness. Just be friendly, polite, and genuine. You can start by asking simple questions, giving compliments, or making small talk. For example, you could ask someone what they're reading, what they do for fun, or what they think of the weather.

Follow up and stay in touch with the people you meet. If you have a good conversation with someone, don't let it end there. Ask for their contact information, such as their phone number, email, or social media. Then, reach out to them and invite them to hang out with you. You can suggest an activity that you both enjoy, such as going to a movie, a coffee shop, or a park.

Be a good friend and show interest in and support for the people you care about. Friendship is a two-way street, so you need to give as well as receive. Listen to your friends when they talk, ask them questions, and offer them advice or help when they need it. Also, remember to celebrate their achievements, cheer them up when they're sad, and have fun with them when they're happy.

I hope these tips help you make new friends and feel less lonely. Remember, you are not alone, and there are many people who would love to be your friends. You just need to put yourself out there and be yourself. I'm sure you'll find some wonderful friends soon.

So, to summarize, this chapter highlights the diverse capabilities of Copilot. It discussed how Copilot can generate image content, demonstrating its creative prowess. It delved into Copilot's ability to translate text, making it an invaluable tool for multilingual communication.

It explored how Copilot can explain various concepts and definitions, acting as a reliable source of information. And it also highlighted how Copilot can provide recommendations based on factual information, thereby aiding the decision-making processes.

Adding a touch of fun to interactions, the chapter revealed how Copilot can generate entertaining content such as jokes, stories, and trivia. It also discusses how Copilot can assist in troubleshooting various issues, showcasing its problem-solving abilities.

Like I've mentioned previously, Copilot's abilities are limitless. It can even offer health-related information based on factual data, assist in planning travel itineraries by providing information on destinations, accommodations, and attractions, and offer support for social interactions by providing conversation starters, etiquette tips, and more.

In essence, this chapter underscores the versatility of Copilot as a tool that can assist in a wide array of tasks, making it a valuable companion for users.

CHAPTER 6

Copilots Adaptive Awareness

Copilot is not just a tool, but a learning genius! In this chapter, we will discover how Copilot fine-tunes its skills with your feedback, generating results that dazzle. Seamlessly aiding writers, it doesn't just suggest sentences or paragraphs — it crafts entire sections of text. With this innovative approach, Copilot elevates the flow, readability, and imaginative flair of written content. For authors, content creators, and communicators, it's an indispensable ally in the quest for captivating and polished work.

However, while it excels in these areas, its efficiency depends on your feedback and interaction. As you interact with Copilot, provide feedback, and incorporate your own suggestions, the AI will learn and adapt to your preferences, giving you more accurate and relevant information over time.

Yet, within its greatness lie some limitations. While Copilot proves to be super beneficial, its suggestions may sometimes not be accurate or align perfectly with your individual preferences. So, you must practice caution and balance the AI's suggestions with critical thinking and verification, especially in some of the more intricate or sensitive contexts.

Despite its incredible potential, Copilot functions as a helper, not a substitute for human knowledge. It recognizes that people's judgment is crucial for difficult tasks and making decisions, showing that human thinking is very important.

Why your Feedback and Preferences are Important

Copilot gets better by learning from the feedback and choices you provide. When you interact with it and let it know what you like or don't like, it adapts and improves based on that information.
Here are some ways that Copilot can learn from your feedback and preferences:

Copilot can learn from your behavior and usage patterns, such as the types of requests you make, the topics you are interested in, the language you use, and the actions you take. It can use this information to understand your context, goals, and preferences and provide you with more relevant and accurate responses.

Copilot can learn from your direct feedback, which leaves no room for misunderstandings, such as ratings, comments, corrections, or suggestions. Copilot uses this feedback to evaluate its performance, identify its strengths and weaknesses, and improve its quality and reliability. You can give feedback to Copilot by clicking on the feedback icon at the bottom of the chat window.

Copilot can learn from your indirect feedback as well; this involves signals, actions, or behaviors that indirectly indicate an individual's thoughts, preferences, or opinions about something.

Indirect feedback can be derived from user behavior, such as clicks, browsing patterns, or interactions, rather than through direct verbal or written communication, the amount of time you spend on a response, the number of times you use a response, or the changes you make to a response. Copilot can use this feedback to measure your satisfaction, engagement, and interest and adjust its responses accordingly.

By learning from your feedback and preferences, Copilot can enhance your creativity, productivity, and enjoyment on the web. Feedback about Microsoft Copilot is collected when you select thumbs-up or thumbs-down on a response from Copilot. After you make your selection, the feedback pane appears and asks for more information — for what you liked (if you selected thumbs-up) or for what went wrong (if you selected thumbs-down). You can offer additional feedback or opt out; it's your choice.

Exploring Copilot Possibilities and Limitations as a Tool

Exploring Copilot's capabilities involves discovering the wide range of tasks it can assist with, such as all the useful abilities I've shared so far in this book. However, it's very important to acknowledge the limitations as well. While it excels in various areas, it might occasionally provide inaccurate suggestions or lack contextual understanding. Understanding these boundaries is key to using Copilot effectively. Some of the possibilities of Copilot are:

-   Event Planning: Copilot can assist in planning events by providing checklists, timelines, and suggestions for venues, themes, and more.

- Recipe Suggestions: Based on dietary preferences or ingredients you have on hand; Copilot can suggest recipes.

- Mental Health Support: Copilot can provide mindfulness exercises, stress relief techniques, and positive affirmations. However, it's important to consult with healthcare professionals for personalized advice.

- Fashion and Style Tips: Copilot can provide fashion and style tips based on the latest trends.

- Home Decoration Ideas: Copilot can provide home decoration ideas based on different styles and spaces.

- Health and Fitness: Copilot can provide information on various exercises, diet plans, and general wellness tips. However, it's important to consult with healthcare professionals for personalized advice.

Some of the limitations of Copilot are

- Microsoft Copilot is a powerful tool with many benefits, but it also has some limitations.

- Privacy Concerns: The AI capabilities of Copilot analyze user data and behaviors to make suggestions, which may raise privacy concerns.

- Learning Curve: Adapting to a new AI-driven workflow can be challenging for some users. The learning curve may slow down the initial application and require training to be able to use Copilot to its full potential.

- Reliance on Technology: While Copilot enhances productivity, it may also lead to a reduced reliance on critical thinking and problem-solving skills, resulting in users' skills becoming rusty.

- Contextual Misunderstandings: Copilot sometimes doesn't understand the context of your prompt and provides suggestions outside of your real intentions.

- Security and Intellectual Property Concerns: Intellectual property concerns could arise in several ways:

Security Concerns

- Data Privacy: AI tools like Copilot analyze user data to make suggestions, which could potentially lead to privacy concerns.

- Inaccurate Information: AI applications may provide answers that sound correct and coherent but are factually wrong.

Intellectual Property Concerns

- Ownership of AI-Generated Works: AI systems are gaining the ability to generate creative works autonomously. This raises critical questions around assigning intellectual property rights (IPR) like copyrights to any of the AI's suggestions or provided answers.

- Use of Training Data: The training data you may use might be copyrighted content; there could be concerns about the use of this content in the training process.

- Plagiarism: There's a risk that AI could inadvertently generate content that closely resembles existing copyrighted content.

To mitigate these risks, it's important for companies that use AI to ensure there in compliance with the law, use training data free from unlicensed content, and develop ways to show ownership, custody, or location of an object of generated content.

It's important to note that these limitations are not unique to Copilot but are common to many AI systems. Users should be prepared for occasional technical hiccups and have backup plans in place.

Remember, it's always important to review any information or suggestion that Copilot provides by cross-checking and verifying its output.

Examples of Useful and Innovative Applications with Copilot

Code completion and generation

- Copilot assists programmers by suggesting code snippets and generating functional pieces of code in various programming languages. This helps streamline development tasks and speeds up the coding process.

For coding assistance

- Copilot can be accessed through supported platforms or integrated into various code editors, like Visual Studio Code. When coding, you can utilize Copilot to get suggestions for code completion, writing functions, fixing errors, or providing examples for specific tasks.

Image creation

- Creating images that are high-quality and accurate to the prompt. Copilot can help you with visual content creation by using AI to generate images based on your description. For example, you can ask it to create an image of a photorealistic dinosaur having its nails attended to by a nail salon.

Research

- It aids in summarizing lengthy texts, condensing information, and assisting with research tasks by providing concise yet comprehensive summaries, saving time for researchers and readers alike.

- Summarizing or asking questions about a video that you are watching in Edge. Copilot can help you understand and learn from videos by providing you with summaries or answers to your queries. For example, you can ask it to summarize a YouTube video of a keynote speech or ask a question about a concept explained in the video.

Creative idea generation

- Creatives and brainstormers find Copilot helpful in sparking new ideas, offering alternative perspectives, and assisting in generating innovative concepts across various creative endeavors.

Content creation and marketing

- Content creators and marketers utilize Copilot for creating engaging content, refining marketing strategies, and generating fresh ideas for campaigns, thereby enhancing audience engagement and outreach.
- Copilot can create a slogan for a new social media platform that specializes in sarcasm. For example, it might suggest "Stratify: The social network that doesn't take itself too seriously" or "Snark: Where sarcasm meets social media.".

Compare

- Copilot can help you go through the pros and cons of making a career change. It can analyze your current and desired jobs, assess your skills and interests, and provide advice on how to make the transition smoothly and successfully.

Organize

- Copilot can create a table that compares top-selling women's running shoes. It can use data from the web to fill in the table with relevant information, such as brand, price, rating, features, and customer feedback.

These applications showcase the broad and significant ways Copilot's capabilities extend across various fields such as writing, coding, academia, business, creativity, design, and more. It also shows Copilot's versatility, usefulness, and efficiency in various tasks and industries.

CHAPTER 7

Making Money with Copilot

In the fast-paced world of tech and coding, tools like Copilot are game- changers. This chapter is all about how you can make money by using your skills and Copilot's abilities. As previously discussed, Copilot isn't just a tool; it's a whole new way of doing things. As people and developers everywhere embrace this cool technology, tons of opportunities are opening for folks who want to make money from what they know.

Here, we'll explore ideas for freelancers, teachers, consultants, and anyone eager to cash in on their skills. Whether you want to teach others, create new tools, or find fresh income streams, this chapter is your guide. The list of potential avenues for making money in this book is diverse and promising.

This chapter, though, is specific to making money using Copilot, and it serves as a guide for you to explore practical plans and pathways that can be put into immediate use, whether you're a developer, entrepreneur, or educator wanting to profitably generate income or create opportunities.

Whichever path you're on and would like to follow further to make money, the insights within this chapter will light the path toward effectively gaining income from your skills and knowledge using Copilot.

Discover how this AI-powered assistant can serve as the starting point for unlocking new realms of success in the ever-changing landscape of software development and entrepreneurial pursuits.

I'm here to also show you how Copilot can help turn your coding skills into cash. Let's dive in and find out how this smart assistant can be your ticket to more success in the coding world and beyond.

Practical Approaches and Opportunities for Action

This refers to practical plans and pathways that can be put into immediate use or implemented to achieve specific objectives or goals. In the context of making money using your skills with Copilot or any technology, practical approaches and opportunities for action represent clear, specific, and actionable steps that individuals or businesses can take to generate income or create opportunities. These strategies and avenues could include:

- Freelancing Services: Offering coding services or projects using Copilot to expedite tasks, thereby taking on more work or attracting more clients.

- Educational Content Creation: Developing courses, tutorials, or blog posts demonstrating how to effectively utilize Copilot, then monetizing these resources through platforms or ad revenue.

- Consulting and Training: Providing consultancy services or hosting training sessions to assist individuals or businesses in integrating Copilot into their workflows, charging fees for these services.

- Creating Tools or Plugins: Developing and selling tools, extensions, or plugins that complement Copilot's functionalities, catering to specific coding needs.

- Contributing to Open Source: Utilizing Copilot to contribute code or solutions to open-source projects, gaining visibility and potential support from the community.

- Building and Selling Applications: Using Copilot to expedite the development process of software applications and monetizing them through sales or licensing agreements.

- Customized Solutions: Offering tailored software solutions to businesses or clients, leveraging Copilot's capabilities, and charging fees for custom development services.

These actionable strategies and ideas provide concrete paths for individuals, entrepreneurs, or developers to utilize Copilot effectively and generate revenue or opportunities based on their expertise and market demand.

Understanding the Legal and Ethical Issues of Using Copilot for Profit

Using Copilot for profit can be a tempting and lucrative option, but it also comes with some legal and ethical challenges that you need to be aware of and address. Here, we will explore some of the key issues that arise when using Copilot for commercial purposes.

By the end of this section, you will have a clear and practical understanding of how to use Copilot for profit in a legal and ethical manner and benefit from its capabilities and features. You will also learn some best practices and guidelines for using Copilot responsibly and effectively. Here is a breakdown of key factors to take into consideration when using copilot to make money:

- Plagiarism and originality: Copilot can help you create content, such as articles, blogs, eBooks, or courses, but you should not claim the output as your own original work. You should also check the output for plagiarism and accuracy and cite your sources properly. You should avoid using Copilot to copy or imitate the work of others or to violate their intellectual property rights.

- Privacy and consent: Copilot can help you communicate and collaborate with others, such as clients, customers, or colleagues, but you should respect their privacy and consent. You should not use Copilot to collect, store, or share personal or sensitive information without permission, or to spam, harass, or deceive others. You should also disclose your use of Copilot and any limitations or uncertainties about the output.

- Fairness and bias: Copilot can help you analyze data, compare products, or find deals, but you should be aware of the potential for unfairness and bias in the output. You should not use Copilot to discriminate, manipulate, or mislead others, or to promote harmful or illegal activities. You should also verify and test the output for validity, reliability, and quality.

To address these considerations, you should:

- Acknowledge and attribute the use of Copilot: You should give proper credit and recognition to Copilot and its sources and avoid passing off the output as your own original work. You should also follow the licenses and terms of use of the code or content that Copilot uses or generates.

- Protect and respect the privacy and consent of others. You should only use Copilot to collect, store, or share personal or sensitive information with permission and in compliance with the applicable laws and regulations. You should also use the guardrails and content filters that Copilot provides and report any inappropriate or harmful output.

- Ensure and evaluate the fairness and bias of the output. You should use Copilot to support, not replace, your own judgment and decision-making, and be transparent and honest about your use of Copilot and its output. You should also review and test the output for accuracy, completeness, and security, and provide feedback to Copilot to help it improve over time.

- Intellectual property rights: Copilot is trained on billions of lines of public code, some of which may be copyrighted or under a restrictive license. If Copilot generates code that matches or resembles the training data, it may infringe on the rights of the original authors. This can expose the users of Copilot to potential lawsuits or claims from the rights holders.

- Quality and reliability: Copilot is not a perfect tool, and it may produce incorrect, incomplete, or insecure code. If the users of Copilot rely on the output without verifying or testing it, they may introduce bugs, errors, or vulnerabilities in their software. This can affect the quality and reliability of their products or services and harm their reputation or customer base.

- Transparency and accountability: Copilot is a black-box system, and it may not be clear how or why it generates certain code. If the users of Copilot do not understand the logic or source of the output, they may not be able to explain or justify their decisions or actions based on the output. This can affect the transparency and accountability of their processes and raise ethical concerns about the trustworthiness and fairness of their software.

To address these issues, the users of Copilot should:

- Respect the intellectual property rights of others: The users of Copilot should check the licenses and terms of use of the code they use or generate with Copilot and comply with them accordingly. They should also give proper credit and attribution to the original authors and avoid copying or plagiarizing their work.

- Verify and test the output of Copilot: The users of Copilot should not blindly accept or use the output of Copilot, but rather review and test it for accuracy, completeness, and security. They should also apply best practices and standards for coding, such as documentation, commenting, and debugging.

- Understand and explain the output of Copilot: The users of Copilot should try to understand the logic and source of the output of Copilot and be able to explain or justify their decisions or actions based on the output. They should also be transparent and honest about their use of Copilot and disclose any limitations or uncertainties about the output.

Platforms and Markets for Copilot Services and Products

The utilization of Copilot services and products spans across various platforms and markets, offering a wide array of opportunities for developers, entrepreneurs, and businesses. Here's an exploration of the diverse platforms and markets where Copilot's services and products find relevance.

Platforms:

- Freelancing Platforms: Websites like Upwork, Freelancer, and Fiverr serve as hubs where developers can offer Copilot-assisted coding services, attracting clients seeking efficient and high- quality coding solutions.

- Educational Platforms: Platforms such as Udemy, Coursera, and Teachable provide avenues for creating courses or tutorials centered around Copilot, catering to individuals eager to enhance their coding skills using this AI tool.

- Tech Forums and Communities: Platforms like Stack Overflow, GitHub, and Dev facilitate discussions, code-sharing, and collaboration, allowing developers to showcase Copilot-generated code, seek feedback, and contribute to open-source projects.

- Marketplaces for Tools and Plugins: Online marketplaces, including the VS Code Marketplace, JetBrains Marketplace, and GitHub Marketplace, enable developers to create and sell extensions, plugins, or tools that complement Copilot's functionalities.

Markets:

- Freelance Services: The freelance market offers significant potential for developers leveraging Copilot to offer coding services. Industries ranging from software development to web design seek efficient solutions, making Copilot-assisted freelancing services highly valuable.

- Education and Training: The education market is vast, where Copilot can be utilized to create coding courses, bootcamps, or workshops. Catering to aspiring developers, students, or professionals seeking to upskill, this market presents opportunities for educational content creators.

- Software Development and Tech Industries: Within these sectors, Copilot can impact the creation of software applications, tools, and products. Companies seeking to streamline development processes or innovate in various tech domains can benefit from utilizing Copilot-assisted coding.

- Open Source and Developer Communities: The open-source market thrives on collaboration, and Copilot's integration into platforms like GitHub fosters community-driven projects. Developers contributing to open-source initiatives leverage Copilot's capabilities to enhance code quality and efficiency.

Cross-Market Opportunities:

- Consulting and Training Services: Developers can tap into multiple markets by offering consulting or training services across industries, helping businesses integrate Copilot into their workflows effectively.

- Custom Solutions: Tailoring Copilot-assisted solutions for specific industries or businesses bridges the gap between different markets, offering customized coding solutions.

Understanding and using Copilot to its maximum advantage in these areas can significantly expand the reach and impact of Copilot services and products, catering to a wide spectrum of users, industries, and development needs.

There are also ways to make money using Copilot using more advanced options, like the ones listed below. I understand this book is for beginner- level learners; I just wanted to offer some other examples beyond just the basic ones. If you want to explore Copilot's abilities further, I've made a list of suggestions on how to do just that.

- Coding: You can use GitHub Copilot to write code faster and better with the help of an AI pair programmer that suggests relevant and high-quality code snippets based on natural language descriptions. You can also use GitHub Copilot X2 to create cross-platform applications with a simple prompt, such as a topic, a document, or a question.

- Office productivity: You can use Microsoft 365 Copilot to create, edit, and share documents, presentations, and spreadsheets with the help of an AI assistant that provides suggestions for content, design, and grammar and allows for real-time collaboration with others. You can also use Copilot in Microsoft Viva4 to learn new skills, access relevant resources, and manage your well-being with the help of an AI coach that guides you through your learning and work journey.

- Web search: You can use Copilot to generate insights, compare products, and find the best deals with the help of an AI analyst that can analyze data, create charts, and provide recommendations.

- Customer service: You can use Dynamics 365 Copilot to provide and fulfill online services for your clients, such as web design, copywriting, editing, proofreading, translation, transcription, data analysis, and more, with the help of an AI agent that can automate or simplify some of the tasks involved in these services, such as generating templates, proposals, invoices, reports, feedback, and more. You can also use Copilot for Service to connect to existing contact centers and CRM solutions and provide personalized and proactive customer service with the help of an AI assistant that can answer questions, resolve issues, and offer solutions.

- Web development: You can use Copilot in Power BI to perform complex data analysis, such as creating charts, tables, formulas, and functions, with natural language commands, with the help of an AI data scientist that can also help you find insights, trends, and patterns from your data and generate summaries and reports. Copilot can also be used in Power Pages to create stunning web pages with a simple prompt, such as a topic, a document, or a question, with the help of an AI web designer that can add relevant content, images, animations, and transitions to your pages and help you design and publish your web pages.

- User interface design: You can use Copilot in Microsoft Fabric to create user interfaces for your applications with the help of an AI UI designer that can generate UI components, layouts, and styles based on natural language descriptions. You can also use Copilot in Microsoft Fabric to test and evaluate your user interfaces with the help of an AI tester that can provide feedback, suggestions, and metrics.

- Operating system: You can use Windows Copilot to customize settings, troubleshoot issues, and connect across your preferred apps with the help of an AI helper that can answer your questions, summarize content, and automate repetitive tasks. You can also use Windows Copilot to enhance your experience with the help of an AI companion that can provide entertainment, education, and inspiration.

I hope you found this list interesting and informative, there are so many more platforms and markets for Copilot's services and products than the ones I've listed for you. I hope you take the time to explore and test out Copilots abilities for yourself. Theres so much more to learn than what I cover in this book.

Successful and Profitable Ventures with Copilot

- Eigen Innovations is a company that uses AI to help car-part makers be more efficient and reduce waste. It uses Copilot to perform complex data analysis and generate insights from sensor data.

- TOMS Shoes is a company that sells shoes and donates a pair to a child in need for every pair sold. It uses Copilot to create and optimize landing pages, write and share product reviews, and create and distribute coupons.

- Microsoft Viva is a platform that helps employees learn new skills, access relevant resources, and manage their well-being. It uses Copilot to provide personalized assistance and feedback and guide users through their learning and work journeys.

- Copilot for Service: A solution that helps businesses provide personalized and proactive customer service. It uses Copilot to create chatbots, email responses, surveys, and more, and connect to existing contact center and CRM solutions.

- Power Pages is a tool that helps users create stunning web pages with a simple prompt. It uses Copilot to add relevant content, images, animations, and transitions to the pages and help users design and publish their web pages.

- Microsoft Fabric is a tool that helps users create user interfaces for their applications based on natural language descriptions. It uses Copilot to generate UI components, layouts, and styles and provide feedback, suggestions, and metrics.

- Windows Copilot is a tool that helps users customize settings, troubleshoot issues, and connect across their preferred apps. It uses Copilot to answer questions, summarize content, and automate repetitive tasks.

- Copilot for Education: A solution that helps educators and learners create and access online courses and content with the help of an AI tutor that can generate topics, outlines, quizzes, and feedback.

- Copilot for Marketing: A solution that helps marketers and businesses create and optimize marketing campaigns and content with the help of an AI copywriter that can generate headlines, slogans, emails, ads, and more.

- Copilot for Design is a solution that helps designers and developers create and test user interfaces and experiences with the help of an AI designer that can generate UI components, layouts, and styles based on natural language descriptions.

- Copilot for Research: A solution that helps researchers and students perform and publish research with the help of an AI researcher that can generate research questions, hypotheses, methods, results, and summaries.

- Copilot for Finance: A solution that helps investors and traders analyze and optimize their financial portfolios and strategies with the help of an AI advisor that can generate insights, recommendations, and reports.

- Freelancing and Coding Services: Freelancing and coding services are some of the ways that you can monetize using Copilot. Copilot can help you write code faster and better with the help of an AI programmer that suggests relevant and high-quality code snippets based on natural language descriptions. You can also use Copilot to create cross-platform applications with a simple prompt, such as a topic, a document, or a question.

  By using Copilot to expedite your coding processes, you can take on more projects, meet tight deadlines, and offer high-quality coding services. This increased efficiency can lead to higher client satisfaction and potentially more lucrative contracts. You can find freelance coders or coding agencies that use Copilot on platforms like Toptal, Upwork, or Fiverr. You can also offer your own freelance or coding services with Copilot on these platforms or on your own website or blog.

- Educational Content Creation: Educational content creation is one of the ways that you can monetize using Copilot. Copilot can help you create online courses, tutorials, or workshops that teach your audience how to use Copilot for various tasks and projects across different domains and applications.

-

    You can use Copilot to generate topics, outlines, quizzes, and feedback for your educational content and to improve your content by adding relevant sources, facts, images, and more. You can then publish or sell your educational content on platforms like Udemy, Coursera, or self-hosted courses.

    By creating educational content with Copilot, you can attract a broader audience eager to learn how to use this AI tool effectively and generate income and growth for your business.

- Tool Development and Marketplaces: Microsoft and OpenAI have announced a joint commitment to support and grow the AI plugin ecosystem for Copilot. Developers can create plugins, extensions, or tools that complement Copilot's features for platforms like Visual Studio Code Marketplace, JetBrains Marketplace, or GitHub Marketplace.

    These plugins can enhance the functionality and usability of Copilot and provide new or improved features for different domains and applications. Successful sales or subscriptions for these tools could lead to profitable ventures, as well as benefit the Copilot community and users.

- Consultancy and Training: Consultancy or training services are some of the ways that you can monetize using Copilot. Copilot can help you provide valuable guidance on AI-driven coding practices to businesses aiming to integrate Copilot into their workflows efficiently. You can use Copilot to demonstrate the capabilities and features of Copilot, such as generating code snippets, creating cross-platform applications, or extending Copilot with plugins and connectors.

You can also use Copilot to teach the best practices and guidelines for using Copilot responsibly and effectively, such as respecting the intellectual property rights of others, verifying and testing the output of Copilot, and understanding and explaining the output of Copilot. By providing consulting or training services with Copilot, you can help businesses adopt, extend, and build Copilot experiences across the Microsoft Cloud and generate income and growth for their own businesses.

You can find potential clients or partners for your consultancy or training services with Copilot on platforms like LinkedIn, Clarity, or Skillshare. You can also offer your own consulting or training services with Copilot on these platforms or on your own website or blog.

To wrap up this section on successful and profitable ventures with Copilot, I have two more final examples:

- Innovation and product Development: It is possible that some companies or individuals could use Copilot to innovate and develop new software applications or tools and then launch them in app stores or via licensing agreements. However, this would depend on several factors, such as the quality, originality, and legality of the code generated by Copilot, the market demand and competition for the applications or tools, and the compliance with the terms and conditions of Copilot and the platforms where they are distributed.

- Contributions to Open Source and Community Impact: Developers contributing high-quality code to open-source projects using Copilot's assistance could gain recognition within the developer community. This recognition might lead to opportunities, collaborations, or even funding for new projects.

It's important to note that while Copilot offers significant potential to enhance efficiency and creativity, the success and profitability of ventures depend on various factors beyond the tool itself. Factors such as market demand, business strategy, marketing efforts, and the quality of the end product or service significantly influence the success of ventures leveraging Copilot.

As Copilot evolves and more developers integrate it into their workflows, we might see more specific and documented instances of successful ventures directly attributed to Copilot's contributions.

Coding Considerations

Copilot is an AI assistant that can help developers write code faster and better by suggesting relevant and high-quality code snippets based on natural language descriptions. Copilot can also help developers learn from the code it generates and improve their coding skills and practices.

However, using Copilot does not automatically guarantee that the code contributed to open-source projects will be high-quality, original, or legal. Developers still need to verify and test the output of Copilot, respect the intellectual property rights of others, and follow the best practices and guidelines for using Copilot responsibly and effectively. Therefore, developers who want to gain recognition within the developer community by contributing high-quality code to open-source projects using Copilot's assistance should:

- Acknowledge and attribute the use of Copilot: Developers should give proper credit and recognition to Copilot and its sources and avoid passing off the output as their own original work. They should also follow the licenses and terms of use of the code or content that Copilot uses or generates.

- Verify and test the output of Copilot: Developers should not blindly accept or use the output of Copilot, but rather review and test it for accuracy, completeness, and security. They should also apply best practices and standards for coding, such as documentation, commenting, and debugging.

- Understand and explain the output of Copilot: Developers should try to understand the logic and source of the output of Copilot and be able to explain or justify their decisions or actions based on the output. They should also be transparent and honest about their use of Copilot and disclose any limitations or uncertainties about the output.

By following these steps, developers can use Copilot to enhance their coding with AI and contribute high-quality code to open-source projects. This could potentially lead to recognition within the developer community and opportunities, collaborations, or funding for new projects.

However, this also depends on other factors, such as market demand and competition for the projects, the quality and relevance of the contributions, and the feedback and reputation of the developers. Again, Copilot is not a substitute for human developers, but rather a tool to augment your own capabilities and creativity.

CHAPTER 8

Unleashing Your Coding Potential

In the realm of coding, Copilot stands as an impressive ally that aids programmers by suggesting code completions, fixing errors, and even generating functional snippets. Its adaptability across multiple programming languages enables it to deliver a wide spectrum of coding needs, helping programmers work more efficiently and get more done.

Coding with Copilot involves utilizing OpenAI's Codex AI model, VS Studio Code, which is a program designed to assist developers by generating code suggestions based on the context provided. Here is a breakdown of essential points about using Copilot and VS Studio Code:

- AI-Powered Assistance: Copilot works within integrated development environments (IDEs) like Visual Studio Code to provide real-time code suggestions. It interprets comments, function names, and context to generate code snippets.

- Language Support: Copilot supports various programming languages, including Python, JavaScript, TypeScript, Ruby, Go, and more. It can help write functions, classes, loops, and other code structures.

- Usage Guidance: To use Copilot effectively, start typing comments or descriptions of the code you want. Copilot will suggest code completions based on this context, which you can accept, modify, or reject.

- Learning Curve: Copilot is not a replacement for learning to code. It is a tool to aid developers by providing suggestions and reducing repetitive tasks. Understanding programming concepts is crucial to making the most of Copilot's suggestions.

- Privacy and Security: Copilot works by training on vast amounts of publicly available code, which raises concerns about code plagiarism, security vulnerabilities, and biased outputs. Exercise caution when using Copilot, review the generated code, and ensure it aligns with security best practices.

- Feedback Loop: Providing feedback to Copilot by correcting its suggestions helps improve its accuracy and relevance over time. This contributes to refining its code-generation capabilities.

- Integration Challenges: While Copilot is a powerful tool, it might not always offer the exact code snippet needed or may suggest inefficient solutions. It is essential to critically assess and adapt the generated code to fit specific project requirements.

- Ethical Considerations: Using Copilot to generate code for proprietary or sensitive projects might raise intellectual property concerns. Understand the legal and ethical implications before using Copilot in commercial or confidential settings.

In summary, Copilot is a valuable coding assistant that can cut your development time by suggesting code snippets based on contextual information. However, it is crucial to use it carefully and thoughtfully, understand its limitations, and complement it with your coding expertise for optimal results.

Here are some steps to get started coding with Copilot

1. Install the GitHub Copilot extension in VS Code. You need an active GitHub Copilot subscription to use it. You can sign up for a free trial from VS Code or from the GitHub Copilot website.

2. Start writing code in your preferred language and framework. Copilot will automatically provide suggestions in gray ghost text. You can accept the suggestions with the Tab key or use the inline suggestion toolbar to switch between multiple options.

3. You can also use Copilot to generate code from natural language descriptions. For example, you can type a comment like // calculate the factorial of n, and Copilot will suggest a function that does that. You can also use Copilot to draft comments and documentation for your code.

4. You can learn from the code that Copilot generates by hovering over it and clicking on the Open in Playground button. This will open a new tab where you can edit, run the code, and see the sources that Copilot used to create it.

5. You can find more information and tutorials on how to use Copilot for various languages and frameworks on the GitHub Copilot website or in the Visual Studio Code documentation. Happy coding!

It's helpful that Copilot can be used with other editors besides VS Code. According to the GitHub Copilot website, Copilot is compatible with:

- Neovim
- JetBrains IDEs,
- especially focused on the latest versions of:
- IntelliJ IDEA
- PyCharm.

To use GitHub Copilot in JetBrains, you must have a compatible JetBrains IDE installed.

- GitHub Copilot is compatible with the following IDEs:
- IntelliJ IDEA (Ultimate, Community, Educational)
- Android Studio
- AppCode, CLion
- Code With Me Guest
- DataGrip
- DataSpell
- GoLand
- JetBrains Client, MPS
- PhpStorm
- PyCharm (professional, community)

You can install the GitHub Copilot extension in your preferred editor and enjoy the benefits of an AI-powered assistant that can generate code, suggest alternatives, and provide documentation based on your natural language input or existing code.

There are very useful extensions you can find in VS Code that can help make your coding experience easier. One very useful extension you need to check out is:

- GitHub Copilot: Your AI pair programmer. Get code suggestions in a real-time IDE. You can start using GitHub Copilot by installing the extension in whichever environment you prefer. If you are not a student, teacher, or maintainer of a popular open-source project, you will be able to take advantage of a 30-day free trial; once that runs out, you will have to purchase a paid subscription for

Using Copilot Offline

Unfortunately, you cannot use Copilot offline. Copilot is a cloud-based service that requires internet access to generate code suggestions based on your input or existing code. Copilot uses a large-scale neural network model that runs on GitHub's servers, and it is not possible to run it locally on your machine. If you need a code completion tool that works offline, you can try other alternatives like TabNine, which uses a smaller and faster model that can be run locally on your machine.

TabNine's default model is hybrid, running both on TabNine's cloud and our user's local machine. TabNine Pro also offers Local Machine Mode, allowing you to run TabNine's AI models locally so your code never leaves your machine.

Please note that on all models, your code and AI training data are never shared or used to train TabNine's public AI model. If you're interested in using TabNine with a specific IDE, you can check out the list of compatible IDEs on their website.

https://www.tabnine.com

TabNine is compatible with a variety of IDEs, including Visual Studio Code, IntelliJ IDEA, PyCharm, and more.
However, Copilot offers more advanced features and supports more languages and frameworks than TabNine. Therefore, if you want to enjoy the full benefits of Copilot, you need to have a stable internet connection.

Is My Code Secure

Your code security is an important aspect of using Copilot. Copilot uses top-notch Azure infrastructure and encryption and an AI-based vulnerability prevention system that blocks insecure coding patterns in real-time. However, Copilot is not a substitute for human review and testing. You should always verify the quality and security of the code that Copilot generates or suggests before using it in your projects.

You should also follow the best practices for secure coding, such as using secure libraries, sanitizing user input, and avoiding hard-coded secrets. Additionally, you should be aware of the intellectual property and privacy implications of using Copilot, as it may use public code or your own code as a basis for providing suggestions. You can find more information and resources on how to responsibly adopt Copilot at the GitHub Copilot Trust Center.

Copilot or Open-Source Projects?

You can use Copilot for open-source projects. You can find more information and resources on how to use Copilot for various languages and frameworks on the GitHub Copilot website:

https://github.com/features/copilot

or the Visual Studio Code documentation:
https://code.visualstudio.com/Docs

There are many popular open-source projects that qualify for free Copilot access. You must have 'write' or admin access to one or more of the most popular open-source projects on GitHub. According to the GitHub Copilot website, some of the criteria for qualifying projects are:

- The project must be licensed under an [OSI-approved license].
- The project must have at least 500 stars on GitHub.
- The project must have had at least 30 contributors in the last year.
- The project must have had at least 10 merged pull requests in the last month.

If you meet these criteria, you can visit the GitHub Copilot subscription page and see if you are eligible for a complimentary subscription. If you are, you can follow the steps to enable GitHub Copilot for your personal account.

You can also use GitHub Copilot for your organization's account if your organization has a GitHub Copilot Business subscription. For more information, you can visit the GitHub Copilot website:

https://github.com/features/copilot

or the GitHub Copilot documentation:

https://docs.github.com/en/copilot

Some examples of popular open-source projects that meet these criteria are:

- [TensorFlow]: free open-source software used for machine learning and AI.

- [Kubernetes]: An open-source system for automating the deployment, scaling, and management of containerized applications.

- [Django]: A high-level Python web framework that encourages rapid development and clean design.

- [Ansible]: A simple, powerful, and agentless tool for automating IT processes.

- [Zulip]: An open-source team chat that helps teams stay productive and focused.

CHAPTER 9

The Future in Coding with Copilot

AI-powered coding tools are software applications that use artificial intelligence (AI) to assist developers in various aspects of programming, such as code completion, generation, debugging, and performance improvement. These tools can help developers write high-quality, scalable code faster, more efficiently, and more creatively. Some examples of AI-powered coding tools are GitHub Copilot, TabNine, Kite, and Codota.

According to some sources, AI-powered coding tools are expected to have a significant impact on the future of programming and software development. Here are some predictions and potential advancements in this field:

- AI-powered coding tools will become more accessible, affordable, and user-friendly, enabling more people to learn and use them for various purposes, such as education, research, and entrepreneurship.

- AI-powered coding tools will become more intelligent, adaptive, and personalized, learning from the user's preferences, habits, and feedback and providing customized suggestions and solutions.

- AI-powered coding tools will become more creative, generative, and collaborative, enabling developers to create novel and innovative applications, products, and services and to work with other developers and stakeholders more effectively.

- AI-powered coding tools will become more ethical, responsible, and secure, ensuring that the code they generate or suggest is accurate, reliable, and safe, and that it respects the user's privacy, intellectual property, and social values.

AI-powered coding tools are an exciting and promising area of AI research and development, and they have the potential to transform the way we program and create software. However, they also pose some challenges and risks, such as the quality and security of the generated code, the intellectual property and privacy implications, and the ethical and social consequences.

Therefore, it is important for developers, researchers, and policymakers to be aware of the opportunities and limitations of AI-powered coding tools and to use them responsibly and wisely.

Several other advancements and trends are anticipated to shape the future of software development. These predictions and potential advancements include:

- Enhanced Contextual Understanding: AI models evolve beyond code completion to better understand project context, user preferences, and specific coding styles, leading to more accurate and personalized code suggestions.

- Expanded Language and Framework Support: Continuous improvements in AI models to encompass a broader range of programming languages, frameworks, and libraries enable developers to work seamlessly across diverse tech stacks.

- Smarter Code Reviews and Debugging: AI algorithms are becoming adept at performing automated code reviews, identifying potential bugs, suggesting fixes, and assisting in debugging processes, thereby streamlining the development lifecycle.

- Collaborative Coding with AI: integration of AI models into collaborative coding environments, fostering team-based development where AI assists in real-time during pair programming or code collaboration.

- Ethical and Security Enhancements: Heightened focus on addressing ethical concerns, ensuring code generated by AI tools meets security standards, and implementing mechanisms to safeguard against potential vulnerabilities and biases.

- AI-Driven Documentation and Knowledge Sharing: AI tools aid in generating documentation, creating tutorials, and facilitating knowledge sharing by automatically extracting information from codebases.

- Customizable and Tailored AI Models: Developers have the ability to fine-tune or train AI models based on specific project requirements, allowing for more customized and domain-specific code generation.

- Integration with Low-Code Platforms: seamless integration of AI- powered coding tools with low-code platforms, enabling rapid development by combining visual interfaces with AI-generated code.

These predictions outline the path that AI-powered coding tools are taking, emphasizing advancements in contextual understanding, broader language support, improved collaboration, ethical considerations, and enhanced developer productivity. As technology evolves, these trends are expected to revolutionize how software is developed, fostering innovation and efficiency in the coding landscape.

Prompts and Queries for Coding

Here are some coding prompts and queries that demonstrate Copilot's abilities to a beginner coding learner:

Basic Function Creation

Prompt:
"Create a function in Python that takes two numbers as input and returns their sum."

Copilot Suggestion:

```python
python Copy code
def add numbers (num1, num2):
return num1 + num2
```

Loop Implementation

Prompt:

"Write a JavaScript loop to print numbers from 1 to 10."
Copilot Suggestion:
JavaScript Copy code

```javascript
for (let i = 1; i <= 10; i++) { console.log(i);
}
```

String Manipulation

Prompt:
"Develop a Python function that reverses a given string."
Copilot Suggestion:
python Copy code

```python
def reverse_string(input_str):
return input_str[::-1]
```

Conditional Statements

Prompt:
"Create a Java program that checks if a number is positive, negative, or zero."

Copilot Suggestion:

java
Copy code

```java
public class NumberCheck {
public static void checkNumber(int num) { if (num > 0) {
System.out.println("Positive");
} else if (num < 0) { System.out.println("Negative");
} else { System.out.println("Zero");
}
}
}
```

List/Array Operations

Prompt:
"Write Python code to find the maximum element in a given list."
Copilot Suggestion:
python Copy code

```python
def find_max(lst): return max(lst)
```

Function Documentation

"Add a comment describing the purpose of a Python function that sorts a list in ascending order."

Copilot Suggestion:

python Copy code

```python
def sort_list(lst):
"""
```

Sorts the given list in ascending order using the default sort() method. Args:
lst: List to be sorted. Returns:
Sorted list. """
lst.sort() return lst

These prompts and Copilot-generated code snippets illustrate how Copilot assists in generating code based on specific instructions or queries, aiding beginners in writing functions, loops, string manipulations, conditional statements, list operations, and even providing documentation for functions in different programming languages.

Using Copilot in different languages and frameworks

Python

You can use Copilot to generate code for common tasks in Python, such as reading and writing files, working with data structures, and creating functions. For example, you can type a comment like # read a csv file into a pandas data frame and Copilot will suggest a code snippet that does that. You can also use Copilot to learn from the code it generates by seeing the sources that it used to create it.

JavaScript:

You can use Copilot to generate code for web development in JavaScript, such as creating elements, adding event listeners, and making API calls. For example, you can type a comment like // create a button element with the text "Click me" and Copilot will suggest a code snippet that does that. You can also use Copilot to suggest alternatives and improvements to your existing code by using the inline suggestion toolbar.

Ruby

You can use Copilot to generate code for Ruby on Rails, a popular web framework that uses Ruby as the programming language. For example, you can type a comment like # generate a model for a blog post with title, content, and author and Copilot will suggest a command that does that. You can also use Copilot to generate code for testing, validation, and authentication in your Rails application.

Go

You can use Copilot to generate code for Go, a fast and simple programming language that is widely used for system programming and web development. For example, you can type a comment like // create a struct for a person with name, age, and address and Copilot will suggest a code snippet that does that. You can also use Copilot to generate code for concurrency, error handling, and networking in Go.

C#

You can use Copilot to generate code for C#, a versatile and powerful programming language that is used for desktop, web, and mobile development. For example, you can type a comment like // create a class for a car with properties for model, color, and speed and Copilot will suggest a code snippet that does that. You can also use Copilot to generate code for inheritance, polymorphism, and generics in C#.

C++

You can use Copilot to generate code for C++, a low-level and high-performance programming language that is used for system programming and game development. For example, you can type a comment like // create a constructor for a circle class that takes the radius as a parameter and Copilot will suggest a code snippet that does that. You can also use Copilot to generate code for pointers, references, and memory management in C++.

These are just some examples of how you can use Copilot to enhance your coding with AI. There are many resources available online to help you learn more about AI-powered coding tools and how to use them effectively. Here are some of the best resources I could find:

- Exploring AI Code: 20 Outstanding AI Code Tools to Accelerate Your Development: This article provides an overview of 20 AI code tools that can help you with various aspects of software development, such as code generation, debugging, testing, and documentation. It also gives some tips on how to choose the right tool for your needs and how to get the most out of them.

https://blog.hubspot.com/website/ai-code

- 14 Best AI Coding Assistant Tools in 2023 (Most Are Free): This article covers 14 AI coding assistant tools that can help you write code faster and more accurately. It explains what each tool does, what we like about it, who it is best for, and how to install and use it.

https://www.elegantthemes.com/blog/wordpress/best-ai-coding-assistant

- 26 AI Code Tools in 2023: Best AI Coding Assistant: This article showcases 26 AI code tools that are transforming the software development landscape by improving efficiency, reducing error rates, and enhancing productivity. It also compares traditional coding tools with AI coding tools and discusses the benefits and challenges of using AI code tools.

https://www.code-intelligence.com/blog/ai-code-tools

- 8 Best AI Coding Tools You Should Use Right Now: This article lists 8 AI coding tools that can generate code, fix bugs, explain code snippets, write unit tests, and more. It also provides some screenshots and videos of how each tool works and how to set it up.

https://beebom.com/best-ai-coding-tools/

CHAPTER 10

Copilot and Microsoft 365

Are you looking for a way to work smarter, faster, and more creatively? Do you want to use the power of AI to transform your productivity and collaboration? If so, you might be interested in Copilot for Microsoft 365, a new tool that can be your AI assistant at work.

Copilot for Microsoft 365 is an innovative solution that combines the power of large language models (LLMs) with your data in the Microsoft Graph and the Microsoft 365 apps to turn your words into the most powerful productivity tool on the planet. Whether you need to write a report, design a presentation, find insights, or communicate with your team, Copilot can help you achieve more with AI.

Copilot for Microsoft 365 is integrated with Microsoft 365 apps, such as Word, Excel, PowerPoint, Outlook, Teams, and others, that can enhance your productivity and creativity. It can also help you create high-quality documents, presentations, reports, and more. You can chat with Copilot using natural language and ask it to complete tasks, generate content, or answer questions for you. Copilot can also suggest relevant information, insights, and actions based on your context and preferences.

Copilot for Microsoft 365 for work is built on Microsoft's commitment to ethical and responsible AI. It includes enterprise-grade security, privacy, compliance, and responsible AI to ensure your data is protected and processed within your Microsoft 365 tenant. You can also customize and control how Copilot interacts with your data and organization.

Copilot for Microsoft 365 for work is not just a tool, but an assistant that works alongside you. It can help you solve complex work tasks, work more productively, and amplify your human creativity. Copilot for Microsoft 365 for work is a whole new way to work with AI.

Features and benefits

Highlighted below are the main features and benefits of Copilot 365 for work.

- AI-powered chat with Microsoft Copilot that can answer your questions, complete tasks, and generate content for you. Here are a few real examples of how you can use AI-powered chat with Copilot:

- If you need to write a report, you can ask Copilot to generate an outline, a summary, or a draft for you. You can also ask Copilot to find relevant sources, data, or images for your report.

- If you need to design a presentation, you can ask Copilot to create a slide deck, a title, or a theme for you. You can also ask Copilot to add animations, transitions, or charts to your presentation.

- If you need to find insights, you can ask Copilot to analyze your data, create a dashboard, or generate a query for you. You can also ask Copilot to visualize your data, filter your results, or compare your metrics.

- If you need to communicate with your team, you can ask Copilot to schedule a meeting, send an email, or create a poll for you. You can also ask Copilot to summarize a meeting, follow up on an email, or share a poll result.

- Integration with Microsoft 365 apps, such as Word, Excel, PowerPoint, Outlook, Teams, and others, that can enhance your productivity and creativity.

- Enterprise-grade security, privacy, compliance, and responsible AI that ensure your data is protected and processed within your Microsoft 365 tenant.

These are many more ways to use Copilot to boost your productivity and creativity at work. You can also explore other scenarios and applications that Copilot can help you with. Just type "help" or "what can you do" to see more options.

How you get started with Copilot and Microsoft 365

- Prerequisites: Before you can access Copilot, you must have the following applications deployed for your work users, which integrate with Microsoft Copilot for Microsoft 365 and other applications: Word, Excel, PowerPoint, Outlook, Microsoft Teams, OneDrive, SharePoint, Exchange.

- OneDrive Account: You need to have a OneDrive account for several features within Microsoft Copilot for Microsoft 365, such as saving and sharing your files.

- New Outlook for Windows: For the seamless integration of Microsoft Copilot for Microsoft 365 with Outlook, you are required to use the new Outlook for Windows.

- Microsoft Teams: To use Microsoft Copilot for Microsoft 365 with Microsoft Teams, you must use the Teams desktop client or web client.

- Microsoft Loop: To use Copilot in Microsoft Loop, you must have Loop enabled for your tenant.

- Microsoft Whiteboard: To use Microsoft Copilot for Microsoft 365 with Microsoft Whiteboard, you must have Whiteboard enabled for your tenant.

- Assign and Manage Licenses: To assign and manage Copilot licenses, you can use the Microsoft 365 admin center.

- Manage Apps with Plugins: Plugins for Copilot are extensions that enable Copilot to access and use third-party apps, such as Jira, Dynamics 365, or Bing Web Search.

Here's an expanded explanation:

Word, Excel, PowerPoint, Outlook: These are essential Microsoft Office applications. Copilot integrates seamlessly with them to provide suggestions and assistance within each application's context. For instance, in Word, it can assist in writing, while in Excel, it aids in calculations, and in PowerPoint, it helps in creating presentations. For Outlook, Copilot can assist in composing emails and managing communication.

Microsoft Teams: Teams is a collaborative platform that allows for communication, file sharing, and collaboration among team members. Copilot's integration with Teams assists users during chats, meetings, and collaborative work by providing real-time suggestions and support.

OneDrive: OneDrive is a cloud storage service that allows users to store and access files from anywhere. Copilot might leverage OneDrive to access and suggest content or information stored there when users are working within the Microsoft 365 ecosystem.

SharePoint: SharePoint is a platform for content management, collaboration, and document sharing within organizations. Copilot's integration with SharePoint could provide assistance in accessing and suggesting relevant documents or information stored within SharePoint sites.

Exchange: Exchange is a messaging platform for emails, calendars, and contacts. Copilot's integration might aid in composing emails, managing schedules, or providing contextually relevant information within Exchange.

How Copilot Integrates with Various Microsoft 365 Apps

- Word: When using Copilot within Word, it assists in suggesting content, phrases, or potential sentence structures as you write. This feature can help enhance your writing process by offering suggestions for more efficient or varied language use.

- Excel: In Excel, Copilot can aid in suggesting formulas, data entry assistance, or even provide explanations for complex functions and calculations, thereby potentially speeding up your workflow and improving accuracy.

- PowerPoint: Copilot integrated with PowerPoint can offer suggestions for slide content, layouts, or assist in creating coherent and impactful presentations by providing content ideas and design suggestions.

- Outlook: Within Outlook, Copilot may assist in composing emails by offering suggestions for text, formatting, or even providing responses based on the context of the email conversation.

- Teams: When integrated with Teams, Copilot can provide real- time assistance during chats, meetings, or collaborative work by suggesting content, responses, or aiding in summarizing discussions.

Overall, Copilot's integration with these Microsoft 365 applications aims to enhance productivity and creativity by providing contextual assistance, suggestions, and support tailored to each application's specific functions and user needs.

The listed applications—Word, Excel, PowerPoint, Outlook, Microsoft Teams, OneDrive, SharePoint, and Exchange—are prerequisites for accessing and effectively utilizing Copilot within the Microsoft 365 environment.

Security and Privacy Concerns

Microsoft Copilot for Microsoft 365 is designed with security and privacy in mind. Here are some key points to consider:

Data Usage

When you enter prompts using Microsoft Copilot for Microsoft 365, the information contained within your prompts, the data they retrieve, and the generated responses remain within the Microsoft 365 service boundary1. This is in keeping with Microsoft's current privacy, security, and compliance commitments.

Data Access

Microsoft Copilot for Microsoft 365 accesses content and context through Microsoft Graph. It only accesses the data to which the user has access.

Compliance

Microsoft Copilot for Microsoft 365 is compliant with existing privacy, security, and compliance commitments to Microsoft 365 commercial customers, including the General Data Protection Regulation (GDPR) and European Union (EU) Data Boundary.

Data Storage

Information about user interactions with Microsoft Copilot for Microsoft 365 is stored1. This data is used to improve the service and provide a better user experience.

Third-Party Plugins

If you're using plugins to help Microsoft Copilot for Microsoft 365 provide more relevant information, check the privacy statement and terms of use of the plugin to determine how it will handle your organization's data.

Public Web Content

If you allow Microsoft Copilot for Microsoft 365 chat experiences to reference public web content, the query sent to Bing might include your organization's data.

Remember, it is important to review the official documentation and stay updated with the latest changes. As new technologies evolve, cyberattacks will increase exponentially, and users' privacy concerns tend to increase. Therefore, understanding how to navigate Copilot's capabilities responsibly is crucial. In summary, to make the most of Copilot within the Microsoft 365 environment, having these applications deployed and accessible to users is crucial.

Copilot's integration with these applications aims to enhance productivity, creativity, and user experience by offering contextual assistance and suggestions tailored to specific tasks within each application. Also, Copilot is designed to protect users' privacy and security, giving you peace of mind that your data is protected.

CHAPTER 11

Best Practices

As Copilot extends its versatile assistance beyond coding, it's crucial to shed light on ethical considerations across various fields. This chapter serves as a compass, guiding individuals — be it researchers, writers, content creators, language translators, and more — through the limitless ways Copilot can be used in many tasks.

This chapter is not only for users in coding but for anyone tapping into Copilot's incredible toolkit. We'll explore the rules and potential issues that arise across different uses, making sure we understand how to navigate Copilot's capabilities responsibly.

We'll discuss how Copilot might present solutions that could unintentionally replicate existing content or pose security concerns, regardless of the field of application. There's also the need to ensure fairness and legality in utilizing Copilot's outputs, be it in written content, image creation, research summaries, or language translations.

This chapter will help you navigate the ethical landscape while using Copilot's diverse functionalities to your advantage. By understanding these ethical considerations, users from various domains can make the most of Copilot's assistance while ensuring integrity, compliance, and fairness in their work.

We're going to cover some of the main issues and challenges that arise from using Copilot, such as intellectual property and privacy, quality and security, bias and ethics, and environmental and social impact. We will also discuss some of the best practices and recommendations for using Copilot responsibly and wisely, and how to avoid or mitigate the risks and harms that may result from using Copilot.

By the end of this chapter, you will have a better understanding of the opportunities and limitations of Copilot, and how to use it in a way that respects the rights, values, and interests of yourself and others.

Ethical Considerations and Potential Pitfalls

- Plagiarism Concerns: Copilot's extensive dataset might inadvertently produce code resembling existing solutions, raising concerns of unintentional plagiarism across various content types like research, writing, or summarization.

- Intellectual Property Issues: Utilizing Copilot-generated content without due diligence might lead to potential infringements on intellectual property rights, especially when using it for creating images, translating content, or writing.

- Security Vulnerabilities: Copilot's suggestions might introduce security loopholes or weaknesses when applied to tasks beyond coding, such as content creation or research, demanding thorough review to ensure data safety and privacy.

- Biased Outputs: Copilot's suggestions could reflect biases present in its training data, affecting outcomes in translations, summarizations, or content creation. Vigilance is necessary to prevent unintentional bias in generated content.

- Licensing and Copyright Compliance: Copilot might propose content that infringes upon licensing agreements or copyrights, necessitating careful consideration and adherence to legal requirements across various applications.

- Quality and Accuracy: Copilot's outputs may not always guarantee accuracy or quality, potentially impacting tasks like translations, image creation, or research summarization. Validation and refinement are essential to ensure precision.

- Privacy Concerns: Content generated by Copilot might inadvertently disclose sensitive or private information, posing privacy risks, especially in areas like content creation or research. Precautions should be taken to safeguard sensitive data.

- Reliance on AI Suggestions: Overdependence on Copilot without comprehensive understanding or critical assessment might impede personal skill development or hinder independent problem-solving abilities.

- Ethical Usage in Decision-making: Ethical dilemmas might arise in scenarios where Copilot's suggestions influence decision-making processes, necessitating a balance between AI assistance and human judgment.

- Legal and Regulatory Compliance: Users must ensure compliance with legal and regulatory frameworks relevant to the specific applications of Copilot, particularly in fields such as content creation, research, or translations.

Navigating these ethical considerations and potential pitfalls demands careful attention, critical thinking, and a proactive approach to ensure responsible, lawful, and ethical use of Copilot's extensive capabilities beyond coding.

But to bring us back to coding with Copilot there are other things to be mindful of while using it for coding tasks, let's look a little deeper into some of these considerations:

- Intellectual property and privacy: Copilot is trained on a large corpus of public code from GitHub, which may include code that is licensed under various terms and conditions. Therefore, the code that Copilot generates or suggests may not be original and may infringe on the rights of the original authors.

  Moreover, Copilot may also use your own code as a basis for providing suggestions, which may raise privacy concerns if you are working on sensitive or confidential projects. You should always review the code that Copilot generates or suggests, and make sure that you have the necessary permissions and attributions to use it in your projects.

- Quality and security: Copilot is not a substitute for human review and testing. The code that Copilot generates or suggests may not be accurate, reliable, or safe, and may contain errors, bugs, or vulnerabilities. You should always verify the quality and security of the code that Copilot generates or suggests and use appropriate tools and practices to ensure that your code meets the standards and requirements of your projects. You should also be careful about the sources that Copilot uses to create the code and avoid using code that comes from untrusted or malicious sources.

- Bias and ethics: Copilot is a product of artificial intelligence, and like any AI system, it may have its own biases and limitations. The code that Copilot generates or suggests may reflect the biases and assumptions of the data that it is trained on and may not be suitable or ethical for certain contexts or applications.

You should try to be mindful of the potential impact and consequences of the code that Copilot generates or suggests and use it responsibly and wisely. You should also be aware of the environmental and social costs of using AI-powered coding tools and strive to use them in a sustainable and inclusive manner.

- Creativity and learning: Copilot can be a great tool for enhancing your creativity and learning, but it can also be a hindrance if you rely on it too much. You should not let Copilot do all the work for you, or copy and paste the code that it generates or suggests without understanding it.

It is best to use Copilot as a guide and a helper, not as a replacement for your own skills and knowledge. You should also challenge yourself to explore new ideas and solutions and not settle for the first or easiest option that Copilot offers.

Security and Privacy Concerns

Reviewing security and privacy concerns while using Copilot involves assessing and addressing potential risks related to data security and user privacy. Here are key considerations:

- Data Privacy: Understand how Copilot processes and stores data. Ensure that sensitive or confidential information isn't shared or inputted into the tool to prevent unauthorized access or misuse.

- User Authentication: Use proper user authentication methods to access Copilot, such as multi-factor authentication, to prevent unauthorized access and enhance security.

- Data Encryption: Confirm that Copilot uses encryption protocols to protect data transmission and storage. Encryption helps safeguard information from unauthorized interception or access.

- Compliance with Regulations: Ensure that the use of Copilot aligns with relevant data protection regulations and compliance standards, such as GDPR (General Data Protection Regulation) or other local privacy laws.

- Monitoring Access: Regularly monitor and control access to Copilot's functionalities. Limit access to authorized personnel and regularly review access logs for any unusual activity.

- Vendor Security Measures: Evaluate the security measures implemented by the Copilot service provider. Check for security certifications, adherence to industry standards, and measures taken to mitigate security threats.

- Data Retention and Deletion: Establish data retention policies to manage the storage and deletion of generated content or user data. Ensure that unnecessary data is promptly deleted to minimize the risk of exposure.

- User Training and Awareness: Educate users on security best practices and potential privacy risks associated with using Copilot. Promote responsible usage and ensure users understand how to handle sensitive information.

- Continuous Risk Assessment: Regularly conduct risk assessments and security audits to identify and address potential vulnerabilities or emerging threats related to Copilot usage.

- Incident Response Plan: Develop an incident response plan outlining steps to be taken in the event of a security breach or privacy incident involving Copilot. This plan should include procedures for reporting, investigating, and mitigating security issues.

By carefully reviewing and addressing security and privacy concerns related to Copilot usage, users and organizations can mitigate risks and ensure a more secure and compliant environment when utilizing the tool.

Conclusion

In conclusion, I hope I've done my duty here today and made you fully aware that Copilot is a powerful and versatile tool that can help you create, learn, and have fun with various types of content. Whether you want to write a poem, code a program, generate an image, or summarize an article, Copilot can assist you with just a few words of input. In this book, you have learned how to use Copilot effectively and efficiently, by following some tips and tricks, choosing the right mode and topic, and experimenting with different prompts and parameters.

You have also seen how Copilot can be used for various purposes, such as fun, learning, and creativity, generating images, stories, jokes, songs, and more. You can also use Copilot to learn new skills, concepts, and languages, and improve your knowledge and understanding. Copilot can be used to unleash your creativity and express yourself in unique and original ways. So let your ideas run free!

But how does Copilot work? How does it produce such amazing and diverse outputs? The answer lies in the power of generative models and neural networks, which are the core technologies behind Copilot. These are advanced artificial intelligence techniques that can learn from large amounts of data and generate new content based on the input and the context. In this book, you have learned the basics of how these techniques work, and how Copilot uses them to create content for you.

You have also learned how to use Copilot for coding, summarizing, and writing, which are some of the most common and useful applications of Copilot. You have seen how it can help you write code in various languages and frameworks, and how it can help you debug, test, and optimize your code. You have also seen how Copilot can help you summarize long texts, articles, and documents, and how it can help you write essays, reports, and books.

But Copilot is not just a passive tool that does what you tell it to do. It's also an active and adaptive tool that can learn from your feedback and interactions. Copilot can adjust its output based on your preferences, goals, and style, and it can also suggest new ideas, options, and improvements for you. In this book, you have learned how to interact with Copilot effectively, and how to provide feedback and guidance to improve its performance and quality.

However, Copilot is not a perfect tool that can do everything for you. It has its own limitations and challenges, and you need to be aware of them and use Copilot responsibly and ethically. In this book, you have learned about some of the potential issues and risks of using Copilot, such as plagiarism, accuracy, bias, and security. You have also learned about some of the legal and ethical implications of using Copilot, such as ownership, rights, and liability.

But this AI technology is also a useful tool that offers many opportunities and benefits for you and others. Copilot can help you make money from your skills and knowledge, by creating and selling products and services based on Copilot's outputs. It can also help you access different platforms and markets for Copilot's services and products, such as online platforms, websites, apps, and games. Copilot can also help you collaborate and communicate with other users and creators, to build a community around Copilot.

Finally, Microsoft's Copilot is a tool that is constantly evolving and improving, and it has huge potential to shape the future of software development and content creation. It's not only a tool for today, but also a tool for tomorrow. Copilot can help you keep up with the latest trends and innovations, and it can also inspire you to create new and novel things. It can also help you learn new things and expand your horizons, challenging you to think critically and creatively.

We can see by this book that Copilot stands as a revolutionary AI-driven tool that opens endless possibilities for creativity, learning, problem-solving, innovation and efficiency. By understanding its capabilities, limitations, and ethical considerations, you can harness its power responsibly unlocking a world of opportunities across various fields and industries. It is a tool that you can use to make a difference in the world.

I hope this book was informative and fun and interesting to read. If you're looking for more of my printed works, you can check out my other books, tailored for the beginner learner just like you. I'm happy you joined me in this informational journey today and hope you continue learning and enjoying good reads in the future. Thank you and take care.

Resources

For Learning More About Microsoft Copilot

Microsoft Copilot-Wikipedia
https://en.wikipedia.org/wiki/Microsoft_Copilot

This is a blog post that explains how to write effective prompts for GitHub Copilot, an AI pair programmer that suggests code snippets based on natural language descriptions.
https://dev.to/github/a-beginners-guide-to-prompt-engineering-with-github-copilot-3ibp

This is a primer that introduces you to Copilot, its capabilities, and how to use it for various coding tasks and projects.
https://education.github.com/experiences/primer_copilot

This is a comprehensive guide that covers the purpose, key features, use cases, and advantages of Copilot.
https://medium.com/@it-craftsman/copilot-for-beginners-everthing-you-need-to-know-9488c37c39a4

This is a tutorial that shows you how to use Windows 11 Copilot, an AI chatbot that can help you perform common tasks and change settings in Windows 11.
https://www.tomsguide.com/how-to/how-to-use-copilot-to-control-windows

This is a support article that welcomes you to Copilot in Windows, an AI chatbot that can help you perform common tasks and change settings in Windows 11. https://support.microsoft.com/en-us/windows/welcome-to-copilot-in-windows-675708af-8c16-4675-afeb-85a5a476ccb0

For Learning More About Copilot and Microsoft 365

This is a learning path that covers the basics, features, and best practices of Copilot for Microsoft 365, a productivity tool that integrates with Microsoft 365 apps and data. https://learn.microsoft.com/en-us/training/paths/get-started- with-microsoft-365-copilot/

This is a learning path that covers the basics, features, and best practices of Copilot for Microsoft 365, a productivity tool that integrates with Microsoft 365 apps and data. https://learn.microsoft.com/en-us/training/paths/get-started- with-microsoft-365-copilot/

This is a web page that highlights the benefits and features of Copilot for Microsoft 365, and how it can help you streamline tasks, automate workflows, and enhance collaboration. https://adoption.microsoft.com/en-us/copilot/

This is a learning article that provides an overview of Copilot for Microsoft 365, its functionality, and its integration with Microsoft Graph and Microsoft 365 apps. https://learn.microsoft.com/en-us/microsoft-365-copilot/microsoft-365-copilot-overview

This is a learning article that introduces the Copilot feature for project management, which can help you generate task plans, assess risks, and create status reports.
https://learn.microsoft.com/en-us/dynamics365/project-operations/project-management/copilot-features

For Learning Ways to Monetize with Copilot

This is a blog post that explores the potential benefits and opportunities of using Copilot for various tasks and projects, such as data analysis, content creation, and customer service.
https://onmsft.com/how-to/7-things-you-can-do-with-microsoft-copilot-and-why-you-should-use-it

This is a blog post that showcases some of the unexpected yet valuable use cases of GitHub Copilot, such as assisting non-native English speakers, creating web pages, and contributing to open-source projects.
https://github.blog/2022-09-14-8-things-you-didnt-know-you- could-do-with-github-copilot/

This is a market analysis that estimates the revenue potential of Copilot for Microsoft, based on different monetization strategies and scenarios
https://markets.businessinsider.com/news/stocks/m icrosoft-has-significant-monetization-opportunity-from-ai-driven-productivity-analysts-1032176553

This is a blog post that announces the support and growth of the AI plugins ecosystem for Copilot, and how developers can create, distribute, and monetize their plugins. https://www.microsoft.com/en-us/microsoft-365/blog/2023/05/23/empowering-every-developer-with-plugins-for-microsoft-365-copilot/

This is a research paper that discusses the ethical and legal implications of GitHub Copilot, and how it can affect the software development industry and society. https://d3.harvard.edu/platform-digit/submission/github-copilot-an-indispensable-game-changer/

For Learning About Copilot Prompts.

This is a support article that explains what Copilot prompts are, how they work, and what you can do with them. https://support.microsoft.com/en-gb/topic/learn-about-copilot-prompts-f6c3b467-f07c-4db1-ae54-ffac96184dd5

This is a support article that explains how to use Copilot Lab, a web app that lets you experiment with Copilot and see how it responds to different prompts. https://support.microsoft.com/en-us/topic/use-copilot-lab-with-a-screen-reader-29bd9822-f68b-4008-8ce8- e2a4cae6adf7

This is a blog post that provides examples and best practices for communicating your desired results to GitHub Copilot, an AI pair programmer that suggests code snippets based on natural language descriptions.

https://github.blog/2023-06-20-how-to-write-better-prompts-for-github-copilot/

For Coding with Copilot, you can Check out These Links

Getting started with GitHub Copilot
https://docs.github.com/en/copilot/using-github-copilot/getting-started-with-github-copilot

The Top AI Code Assistant Tools of 2023
https://topaitools.com/articles/the-top-ai-code-assistant-tools

This is a blog post that provides examples and best practices for communicating your desired results to GitHub Copilot, an AI pair programmer that suggests code snippets based on natural language descriptions.
https://github.blog/2023-06-20-how-to-write-better-prompts-for-github-copilot/

GitHub Copilot in VS Code
https://code.visualstudio.com/docs/editor/github-copilot

The world's most widely adopted AI developer tool.
https://github.com/features/copilot

Cited Websites

Microsoft Copilot in Edge
https://learn.microsoft.com/en-us/copilot/edge

Microsoft Edge, features and tips for Copilot
https://www.microsoft.com/en-us/edge/features/copilot?form=MA13FJ

Bing Chat is now Microsoft Copilot: What's new and is it better than ChatGPT?
https://www.androidauthority.com/microsoft-copilot-3386321/

Wiki how- How to Have a Balanced Life
https://www.wikihow.com/Have-a-Balanced-Life

Tips for Finding your Work/School/Life Balance
https://www.uoguelph.ca/oac/news/tips-finding-your-workschoollife-balance

Unlocking Why Work Life Balance Is Important for Professionals (10 Reasons)
https://www.coursecorrectioncoaching.com/why-work-life-balance-is-important/

Self-Development: The 9 Skills You Need to Improve Your Life https://www.berkeleywellbeing.com/self-development-the-9-skills-you-need-to-improve-your-life.html

What will you do with Copilot in Bing?
https://www.microsoft.com/en-us/bing?ep=251&es=31&form=MA13FV

Using Copilot AI Assistant in Edge Browser
https://softtuts.com/copilot-ai-assistant-in-edge-browser/

Microsoft Copilot AKA Bing AI: Navigating Through Inaccuracies and Limitations
https://original.newsbreak.com/@760-news-1797443/3255426568175-microsoft-copilot-aka-bing-ai-navigating-through-inaccuracies-and-limitations

Microsoft Bing blogs
https://blogs.bing.com/search-quality-insights/december-2023/Continued-AI-Innovation-in-Copilot

7 uses of Microsoft 365 Copilot to improve productivity
https://openaimaster.com/7-uses-of-microsoft-365-copilot- to-improve-productivity/

Five of the Most Intriguing 365 Copilot Use Cases
https://www.uctoday.com/collaboration/five-of-the-most-intriguing-365-copilot-use-cases/

What are Microsoft's different Copilots? Here's what they are and how you can use them
https://www.zdnet.com/article/what-is-microsoft-copilot-heres-everything-you-need-to-know/

How to use Windows 11 Copilot — here's what you can do with AI https://www.tomsguide.com/how-to/how-to-use-copilot-to-control-windows

Make the everyday easier
https://www.microsoft.com/en-us/windows?wa=wsignin1.0

7 things you can do with Microsoft Copilot and why you should use it
https://onmsft.com/how-to/7-things-you-can-do-with-microsoft-copilot-and-why-you-should-use-it/

Microsoft 365 Copilot: Prompting Do's and Don'ts
https://adoption.microsoft.com/files/copilot/Prompt-dos-and-donts-one-pager.pdf

8 things you didn't know you could do with GitHub Copilot
https://github.blog/2022-09-14-8-things-you-didnt-know-you- could-do-with-github-copilot/

Get the most out of generative AI for your startup with Microsoft Copilot
https://startups.microsoft.com/blog/get-the-most-out-of-generative-ai-for-your-startup-with-microsoft-copilot/

How to Use Windows Copilot to Summarize a Webpage
https://nerdschalk.com/how-to-use-windows-copilot-to-summarize-a-webpage/

Window 11 Copilot: 10 Best tips and tricks
https://pureinfotech.com/window-11-copilot-best-tips-tricks/

What Are Keywords? (and Why You Need to Know How to Find The.
https://blog.hubspot.com/marketing/keywords

Give security teams an edge with Microsoft Security Copilot
https://www.microsoft.com/en-us/security/business/ai-machine-learning/microsoft-security-copilot

Copilot Review: Use AI To Understand Your Spending and Income
https://thecollegeinvestor.com/41976/copilot-review/

FAQ for Copilot data security and privacy in Microsoft Power Platform
https://learn.microsoft.com/en-us/power-platform/faqs-copilot-data-security-privacy

GitHub Copilot: Revolutionizing Code Generation with AI-Powered Assistance
https://kodekloud.com/blog/github-copilot/

The Power of Understanding Context: How It Can Improve Your Communication Skills
https://oboloo.com/blog/the-power-of-understanding-context-how-it-can-improve-your-communication-skills/

Research: quantifying GitHub Copilot's impact on developers productivity and happiness
https://github.blog/2022-09-07-research-quantifying-github-copilots-impact-on-developer-productivity-and-happiness/

5 Ways to Make Your Chatbot More Contextually Intelligent
https://verloop.io/blog/contextual-chatbot/

Tips for using privacy settings
https://www.priv.gc.ca/en/privacy-topics/technology/online-privacy-tracking-cookies/online-privacy/gd_ps_201903/?WT.ac=set-en-1

Data, Privacy, and Security for Microsoft Copilot for Microsoft 365
https://learn.microsoft.com/en-us/microsoft-365-copilot/microsoft-365-copilot-privacy

What Good Feedback Really Looks Like
https://hbr.org/2019/05/what-good-feedback-really-looks-like

Protecting Yourself in the Digital Age: Common Cybersecurity Threats and How to Stay
https://www.mcgill.ca/cybersafe/article/protecting-yourself- digital-age-common-cybersecurity-threats-and-how-stay-safe

Introducing Microsoft Copilot Studio and new features in Copilot for Microsoft 365
https://www.microsoft.com/en-us/microsoft-365/blog/2023/11/15/introducing-microsoft-copilot-studio-and-new-features-in-copilot-for-microsoft-365/

GitHub Copilot – August 28th Update
https://github.blog/changelog/2023-08-28-github-copilot-august-28th-update/

About the Author

I am a mom of four, a creative explorer, and an unwavering believer in the power of AI to transform everyday life. When I discovered Microsoft Copilot, it wasn't just another tech tool — it became my brainstorming partner, research assistant, and even a co-creator of AI-generated animations. With no formal tech background but endless curiosity, I dove headfirst into mastering Copilot's limitless possibilities, from engineering perfect prompts to streamlining tasks for my future online business.

Inspired by how Copilot helped me think bigger, I wrote "*The #1 Book to Learn Microsoft Copilot*" to give beginners the same "*Aha!*" moments I experienced. My mission? To prove that AI isn't just for coders — it's for moms, dreamers, and anyone ready to work smarter.

When not testing Copilot's latest features (or eagerly awaiting my new Copilot PC), I'm either working on my next beginner-friendly guide, sweating it out in a workout session, or savoring the chaos and joy of family life.

I'm also the author of "*The #1 Book to Learn Kindness and Caring*" and "*The #1 Book to Learn Habit Mastery*" — because whether it's tech, personal growth, or simply living well, I'm all about unlocking potential.

Join me on this AI journey!

Https://www.amazon.com/author/heathermatalski

Instagram@Authorheathermatalski

TikTok@Authorheathermatalski

Email matalski.heather@outlook.com

Please check me out on my social media and if you like this book, please leave me a review on Amazon and let me know your thoughts on it.

Thank you so much for your support!!

www.ingramcontent.com/pod-product-compliance
Lightning Source LLC
Chambersburg PA
CBHW071002050326
40689CB00014B/3452